"Bracing."   —*The Nation*

"Reading Harris's *Letter to a Christian Nation* was like sitting ringside, cheering the champion, yelling 'Yes!' at every jab. For those of us who feel depressed by this country's ever increasing unification of church and state, and the ever decreasing support for the sciences that deliver knowledge and reduce ignorance, this little book is a welcome hit of adrenalin."
—Marc Hauser, Professor of Psychology, Biology, and Biological Anthropology at Harvard University, author of *Moral Minds*

"Sam Harris's elegant little book is most refreshing and a wonderful source of ammunition for those who, like me, hold to no religious doctrine. Yet I have some sympathy also with those who might be worried by his uncompromising stance. Read it from your own view, but do not ignore its message."
—Sir Roger Penrose, Emeritus Professor of Mathematics, Oxford University, author of *The Road to Reality*

"Read this book and decide your stance for the future."
—Michael S. Gazzaniga, Director of
the Sage Center for the Study of Mind,
University of California, Santa Barbara,
author of *The Ethical Brain*

"Sam Harris fearlessly describes a moral and intellectual emergency precipitated by religious fantasies—misguided beliefs that create suffering, that rationalize violence, that have endangered our nation and our future. . . . Now when the subject arises, as it inevitably does, I can simply say: Read Sam Harris's *Letter to a Christian Nation*."
—Janna Levin, Columbia University, author of
How the Universe Got Its Spots and
A Madman Dreams of Turing Machines

"If you believe in a religion, even the mildest form of Christianity, please read this book. It won't take you long, but it might change your mind."
—Matt Ridley, author of *Genome* and
Nature Via Nurture

SAM HARRIS

Letter to a Christian Nation

Sam Harris is the author of the *New York Times*
bestseller *The End of Faith: Religion, Terror, and
the Future of Reason,* winner of the 2005 PEN/
Martha Albrand Award for First Nonfiction.

ALSO BY SAM HARRIS

The End of Faith: Religion, Terror,
and the Future of Reason

Letter to a
Christian Nation

Letter to a
Christian Nation

SAM HARRIS

VINTAGE BOOKS
A Division of Random House, Inc.
New York

The Library of Congress has cataloged the Knopf edition as follows:
Harris, Sam, [date].
Letter to a Christian nation / Sam Harris.— 1st ed.
p.   cm.
1. Christianity and politics—United States.   2. Church and state—
United States.   3. Fundamentalism—United States.   4. Religious
right—United States.   5. Christian conservatism—United States.
I. Title.
BR516.H255   2006
277.3'083—dc22
2006046578

Vintage ISBN: 978-0-307-27877-7

Book design by Virginia Tan

www.vintagebooks.com

Printed in the United States of America
10   9   8   7   6   5

For my wife

NOTE TO THE READER

SINCE the publication of my first book, *The End of Faith*, thousands of people have written to tell me that I am wrong not to believe in God. The most hostile of these communications have come from Christians. This is ironic, as Christians generally imagine that no faith imparts the virtues of love and forgiveness more effectively than their own. The truth is that many who claim to be transformed by Christ's love are deeply, even murderously, intolerant of criticism. While we may want to ascribe this to human nature, it is clear that such hatred draws considerable support from the Bible. How do I know this? The most disturbed of my correspondents always cite chapter and verse.

While this book is intended for people of

all faiths, it has been written in the form of a letter to a Christian. In it, I respond to many of the arguments that Christians put forward in defense of their religious beliefs. The primary purpose of the book is to arm secularists in our society, who believe that religion should be kept out of public policy, against their opponents on the Christian Right. Consequently, the "Christian" I address throughout is a Christian in a narrow sense of the term. Such a person believes, at a minimum, that the Bible is the inspired word of God and that only those who accept the divinity of Jesus Christ will experience salvation after death. Dozens of scientific surveys suggest that well over half of the American population subscribes to these beliefs. Of course, such metaphysical commitments do not imply any particular denomination of Christianity. Conservatives in every sect—Catholics, mainline Protestants, Evangelicals, Baptists, Pentecostals, Jehovah's Witnesses, and so on—are equally implicated in my argument. As is well known, the beliefs of conservative Christians now exert an extraordinary influence over our national discourse—

in our courts, in our schools, and in every branch of government.

In *Letter to a Christian Nation,* I have set out to demolish the intellectual and moral pretensions of Christianity in its most committed forms. Consequently, liberal and moderate Christians will not always recognize themselves in the "Christian" I address. They should, however, recognize one hundred and fifty million of their neighbors. I have little doubt that liberals and moderates find the eerie certainties of the Christian Right to be as troubling as I do. It is my hope, however, that they will also begin to see that the respect they demand for their own religious beliefs gives shelter to extremists of all faiths. Although liberals and moderates do not fly planes into buildings or organize their lives around apocalyptic prophecy, they rarely question the legitimacy of raising a child to believe that she is a Christian, a Muslim, or a Jew. Even the most progressive faiths lend tacit support to the religious divisions in our world. In *Letter to a Christian Nation,* however, I engage Christianity at its most divisive, injurious, and retrograde. In this, liberals, moderates, and nonbelievers can recognize a common cause.

ACCORDING to a recent Gallup poll, only 12 percent of Americans believe that life on earth has evolved through a natural process, without the interference of a deity. Thirty-one percent believe that evolution has been "guided by God." If our worldview were put to a vote, notions of "intelligent design" would defeat the science of biology by nearly three to one. This is troubling, as nature offers no compelling evidence for an intelligent designer and countless examples of *un*intelligent design. But the current controversy over "intelligent design" should not blind us to the true scope of our religious bewilderment at the dawn of the twenty-first century. The same Gallup poll revealed that 53 percent of Americans are actually *creationists*. This means that despite a full century of scientific insights attesting to the antiquity of life and the greater antiquity of the earth, more than half of our neighbors believe that the entire cosmos was created six thousand years ago. This is, incidentally, about a thousand years after the Sumerians invented glue. Those with the power to elect our presidents and congressmen—and many who themselves get elected—believe that dinosaurs lived two by two upon Noah's ark, that light from distant galaxies was created en route to the earth, and that the first members of our species were fashioned out of dirt and divine breath, in a garden with a talking snake, by the hand of an invisible God.

Among developed nations, America stands alone in these convictions. Our country now appears, as at no other time in her history, like a lumbering, bellicose, dim-witted giant. Anyone who cares about the fate of civilization would do well to recognize that the combination of great power and great stupidity is simply terrifying, even to one's friends.

The truth, however, is that many of us may not care about the fate of civilization. Forty-four percent of the American population is convinced that Jesus will return to judge the living and the dead *sometime in the next fifty years.* According to the most common interpretation of biblical prophecy, Jesus will return only after things have gone horribly awry here on earth. It is, therefore, not an exaggeration to say that if the city of New York were suddenly replaced by a ball of fire, some significant percentage of the American population would see a silver lining in the subsequent mushroom cloud, as it would suggest to them that the best thing that is ever going to happen was about to happen: the return of Christ. It should be blindingly obvious that beliefs of this sort will do little to help us create a durable future for ourselves—socially, economically, environmentally, or geopolitically. Imagine the consequences if any significant component of the U.S. government actually believed that the world was about to end and that its ending would be *glorious*. The fact that nearly half of the American population apparently believes this, purely on the basis of religious dogma, should be considered a moral and intellectual emergency. The book you are about to read is my response to this emergency. It is my sincere hope that you will find it useful.

Sam Harris
May 1, 2006
New York

*Letter to a
Christian Nation*

YOU BELIEVE that the Bible is the word of God, that Jesus is the Son of God, and that only those who place their faith in Jesus will find salvation after death. As a Christian, you believe these propositions not because they make you feel good, but because you think they are true. Before I point out some of the problems with these beliefs, I would like to acknowledge that there are many points on which you and I agree. We agree, for instance, that if one of us is right, the other is wrong. The Bible is either the word of God, or it isn't. Either Jesus offers humanity the one, true path to salvation (John 14:6), or he does not. We agree that to be a true Christian is to believe that all other faiths are mistaken, and profoundly so. If Christianity is correct, and I persist in my unbelief, I should expect to suffer the torments of hell. Worse still, I have persuaded others, and many close to me, to reject the very idea of God. They too will languish in "eternal fire" (Matthew 25:41). If the basic doctrine of Christianity is correct, I have misused my life in the worst conceivable way. I admit this without a single caveat. The fact that my continuous and public rejection of Christianity does not worry me in the least should suggest to you just how inadequate I think your reasons for being a Christian are.

Of course, there are Christians who do not agree with either of us. There are Christians who consider other faiths to be equally valid paths to salvation. There are Christians who have no fear of hell and who do not believe in the physical resurrection of Jesus. These Christians often describe themselves as "religious liberals" or "religious moderates." From their point of view, you and I have both misunderstood what it means to be a person of faith. There is, we are assured, a vast and beautiful terrain between atheism and religious fundamentalism that generations of thoughtful Christians have quietly explored. According to liberals and moderates, faith is about mystery, and meaning, and community, and love. People make religion out of the full fabric of their lives, not out of mere beliefs.

I have written elsewhere about the problems I see with religious liberalism and religious moderation. Here, we need only observe that the issue is both simpler and more urgent than liberals and moderates generally admit. Either the Bible is just an ordinary book, written by mortals, or it isn't. Either Christ was divine, or he was not. If the Bible is an ordinary book, and Christ an ordinary man, the basic doctrine of Christianity is false. If the Bible is an ordinary book, and Christ an ordinary man, the history of Christian theology is the story of bookish men parsing a collective delusion. If the basic tenets of Christianity are true, then there are some very grim surprises in store for nonbelievers like myself. You understand this. At least half of the American population understands this. So let us be honest with ourselves: in the fullness of time, one side is really going to win this argument, and the other side is really going to lose.

. . .

CONSIDER: every devout Muslim has the same reasons for being a Muslim that you have for being a Christian. And yet you do not find their reasons compelling. The Koran repeatedly declares that it is the perfect word of the creator of the universe. Muslims believe this as fully as you believe the Bible's account of itself. There is a vast literature describing the life of Muhammad that, from the point of view of Islam, proves that he was the most recent Prophet of God. Muhammad also assured his followers that Jesus was *not* divine (Koran 5:71–75; 19:30–38) and that anyone who believes otherwise will spend eternity in hell. Muslims are certain that Muhammad's opinion on this subject, as on all others, is infallible.

Why don't you lose any sleep over whether to convert to Islam? Can you prove that Allah is not the one, true God? Can you prove that the archangel Gabriel did not visit Muhammad in his cave? Of course not. But you need not prove any of these things to reject the beliefs of Muslims as absurd. The burden is upon them to prove that their beliefs about God and Muhammad are valid. They have not done this. They cannot do this. Muslims are simply not making claims about reality that can be corroborated. This is perfectly apparent to anyone who has not anesthetized himself with the dogma of Islam.

The truth is, you know exactly what it is like to be an atheist with respect to the beliefs of Muslims. Isn't it obvious that Muslims are fooling themselves? Isn't it obvious that anyone who thinks that the Koran is the perfect word of the creator of the universe has not read the book critically? Isn't it obvious that the doctrine of Islam represents a near-perfect barrier to honest inquiry? Yes, these things are obvious. Understand that the way you view Islam is precisely the way devout Muslims view Christianity. And it is the way I view all religions.

The Wisdom of the Bible

You believe that Christianity is an unrivaled source of human goodness. You believe that Jesus taught the virtues of love, compassion, and selflessness better than any teacher who has ever lived. You believe that the Bible is the most profound book ever written and that its contents have stood the test of time so well that it must have been divinely inspired. All of these beliefs are false.

Questions of morality are questions about happiness and suffering. This is why you and I do not have moral obligations toward rocks. To the degree that our actions can affect the experience of other creatures positively or negatively, questions of morality apply. The idea that the Bible is a perfect guide to morality is simply astounding, given the contents of the book. Admittedly, God's counsel to parents is straightforward: whenever children get out of line, we should beat them with a rod (Proverbs 13:24, 20:30, and 23:13–14). If they are shameless enough to talk back to us, we should kill them (Leviticus 20:9, Deuteronomy 21:18–21, Mark 7:9–13, and Matthew 15:4–7). We must also stone people to death for heresy, adultery, homosexuality, working on the Sabbath, worshipping graven images, practicing sorcery, and a wide variety of other imaginary crimes. Here is just one example of God's timeless wisdom:

> *If your brother, the son of your mother, or*
> *your son, or your daughter, or the wife of*
> *your bosom, or your friend who is as your*

own soul, entices you secretly, saying, "Let us go and serve other gods," . . . you shall not yield to him or listen to him, nor shall your eye pity him, nor shall you spare him, nor shall you conceal him; but you shall kill him; your hand shall be first against him to put him to death, and afterwards the hand of all the people. You shall stone him to death with stones, because he sought to draw you away from the LORD your God, who brought you out of the land of Egypt, out of the house of bondage. . . . If you hear in one of your cities, which the LORD your God gives you to dwell there, that certain base fellows have gone out among you and have drawn away the inhabitants of the city, saying, "Let us go and serve other gods," which you have not known, then you shall inquire and make search and ask diligently; and behold, if it be true and certain that such an abominable thing has been done among you, you shall surely put the inhabitants of that city to the sword, destroying it utterly, all who are in it and its cattle, with the edge of the sword.

—DEUTERONOMY 13:6, 8–15

Many Christians believe that Jesus did away with all this barbarism in the clearest terms imaginable and delivered a doctrine of pure love and toleration. He didn't. In fact, at several points in the New Testament, Jesus can be read to endorse the entirety of Old Testament law.

> For truly, I say to you, till heaven and earth pass away, not an iota, not a dot, will pass from the law until all is accomplished. Whoever then relaxes one of the least of these commandments and teaches men so, shall be called least in the kingdom of heaven; but he who does them and teaches them shall be called great in the kingdom of heaven. For I tell you, unless your righteousness exceeds that of the scribes and Pharisees, you will never enter the kingdom of heaven.
>
> —MATTHEW 5:18–20

The apostles regularly echo this theme (for example, see 2 Timothy 3:16–17). It is true, of course, that Jesus said some profound things about love and charity and forgiveness. The

Golden Rule really is a wonderful moral precept. But numerous teachers offered the same
instruction centuries before Jesus (Zoroaster,
Buddha, Confucius, Epictetus . . .), and countless scriptures discuss the importance of self-
transcending love more articulately than the
Bible does, while being unblemished by the
obscene celebrations of violence that we find
throughout the Old and New Testaments. If
you think that Christianity is the most direct
and undefiled expression of love and compassion the world has ever seen, you do not know
much about the world's other religions.

Take the religion of Jainism as one example.
The Jains preach a doctrine of utter nonviolence. While the Jains believe many improba-
ble things about the universe, they do not
believe the sorts of things that lit the fires of
the Inquisition. You probably think the Inquisition was a perversion of the "true" spirit of
Christianity. Perhaps it was. The problem, however, is that the teachings of the Bible are so
muddled and self-contradictory that it was
possible for Christians to happily burn heretics
alive for five long centuries. It was even possible for the most venerated patriarchs of the

Church, like St. Augustine and St. Thomas Aquinas, to conclude that heretics should be tortured (Augustine) or killed outright (Aquinas). Martin Luther and John Calvin advocated the wholesale murder of heretics, apostates, Jews, and witches. You are, of course, free to interpret the Bible differently—though isn't it amazing that you have succeeded in discerning the true teachings of Christianity, while the most influential thinkers in the history of your faith failed? Of course, many Christians believe that a harmless person like Martin Luther King, Jr., is the best exemplar of their religion. But this presents a serious problem, because the doctrine of Jainism is an objectively better guide for becoming like Martin Luther King, Jr., than the doctrine of Christianity is. While King undoubtedly considered himself a devout Christian, he acquired his commitment to nonviolence primarily from the writings of Mohandas K. Gandhi. In 1959, he even traveled to India to learn the principles of nonviolent social protest directly from Gandhi's disciples. Where did Gandhi, a Hindu, get his doctrine of nonviolence? He got it from the Jains.

If you think that Jesus taught only the Golden Rule and love of one's neighbor, you should reread the New Testament. Pay particular attention to the morality that will be on display when Jesus returns to earth trailing clouds of glory:

> *God deems it just to repay with affliction those who afflict you . . . when the Lord Jesus is revealed from heaven with his mighty angels in flaming fire, inflicting vengeance upon those who do not know God and upon those who do not obey the gospel of our Lord Jesus. They shall suffer the punishment of eternal destruction and exclusion from the presence of the Lord and from the glory of his might . . .*
>
> —2 THESSALONIANS 1:6–9

> *If a man does not abide in me, he is cast forth as a branch and withers; and the branches are gathered, thrown into the fire and burned.*
>
> —JOHN 15:6

If we take Jesus in half his moods, we can easily justify the actions of St. Francis of Assisi or Martin Luther King, Jr. Taking the other half, we can justify the Inquisition. Anyone who believes that the Bible offers the best guidance we have on questions of morality has some very strange ideas about either guidance or morality.

IN ASSESSING the moral wisdom of the Bible, it is useful to consider moral questions that have been solved to everyone's satisfaction. Consider the question of slavery. The entire civilized world now agrees that slavery is an abomination. What moral instruction do we get from the God of Abraham on this subject? Consult the Bible, and you will discover that the creator of the universe clearly expects us to keep slaves:

> As for your male and female slaves whom
> you may have: you may buy male and
> female slaves from among the nations that
> are round about you. You may also buy
> from among the strangers who sojourn

with you and their families that are with
you, who have been born in your land; and
they may be your property. You may
bequeath them to your sons after you, to
inherit as a possession forever; you may
make slaves of them, but over your
brethren the people of Israel you shall not
rule, one over another, with harshness.

—LEVITICUS 25:44–46

The Bible also makes it clear that every man is free to sell his daughter into sexual slavery— though certain niceties apply:

When a man sells his daughter as a slave,
she shall not go out as the male slaves do. If
she does not please her master, who has
designated her for himself, then he shall let
her be redeemed; he shall have no right to
sell her to a foreign people, since he has
dealt faithlessly with her. If he designates
her for his son, he shall deal with her as
with a daughter. If he takes another wife to
himself, he shall not diminish her food, her
clothing, or her marital rights. And if he

*does not do these three things for her, she
shall go out for nothing, without payment
of money.*

—EXODUS 21:7–11

The only real restraint God counsels on the subject of slavery is that we not beat our slaves so severely that we injure their eyes or their teeth (Exodus 21). It should go without saying that is not the kind of moral insight that put an end to slavery in the United States.

There is no place in the New Testament where Jesus objects to the practice of slavery. St. Paul even admonishes slaves to serve their masters well—and to serve their Christian masters especially well:

*Slaves, be obedient to those who are your
earthly masters, with fear and trembling,
in singleness of heart, as to Christ. . . .*

—EPHESIANS 6:5

*Let all who are under the yoke of slavery
regard their masters as worthy of all honor,*

*so that the name of God and the teaching
may not be defamed. Those who have
believing masters must not be disrespectful
on the ground that they are brethren;
rather they must serve all the better since
those who benefit by their service are
believers and beloved. Teach and urge
these duties. If any one teaches otherwise
and does not agree with the sound words of
our Lord Jesus Christ and the teaching
which accords with godliness, he is puffed
up with conceit, he knows nothing; he has
a morbid craving for controversy and for
disputes about words, which produce envy,
dissension, slander, base suspicions . . .*

—1 TIMOTHY 6:1–4

It should be clear from these passages that, while the abolitionists of the nineteenth century were morally right, they were on the losing side of a theological argument. As the Reverend Richard Fuller put it in 1845, "What God sanctioned in the Old Testament, and permitted in the New, cannot be a sin." The good Reverend was on firm ground here. Nothing in Christian theology remedies the appalling deficiencies of the Bible on what is perhaps the greatest—and the *easiest*—moral question our society has ever had to face.

In response, Christians like yourself often point out that the abolitionists also drew considerable inspiration from the Bible. Of course they did. People have been cherry-picking the Bible for millennia to justify their every impulse, moral and otherwise. This does not mean, however, that accepting the Bible to be the word of God is the best way to discover that abducting and enslaving millions of innocent men, women, and children is morally wrong. It clearly isn't, given what the Bible actually says on the subject. The fact that some abolitionists used parts of scripture to repudiate other parts does not indicate that the Bible is a good guide to morality. Nor does it suggest that human beings should need to consult a book in order to resolve moral questions of this sort. The moment a person recognizes that slaves are human beings like himself, enjoying the same capacity for suffering and happiness, he will understand that it is patently evil to own them and treat them like farm equipment. It is remarkably easy for a person to arrive at this epiphany—and yet, it had to be spread at the point of a bayonet throughout the Confederate South, among the most pious Christians this country has ever known.

THE TEN COMMANDMENTS are also worthy of some reflection in this context, as most Americans seem to think them both morally and legally indispensable. While the U.S. Constitution does not contain a single mention of God, and was widely decried at the time of its composition as an irreligious document, many Christians believe that our nation was founded on "Judeo-Christian principles." Strangely, the Ten Commandments are often cited as incontestable proof of this fact. While their relevance to U.S. history is questionable, our reverence for the commandments is not an accident. They are, after all, the only passages in the Bible so profound that the creator of the universe felt the need to physically write them himself—

and in stone. As such, one would expect these to be the greatest lines ever written, on any subject, in any language. Here they are. Get ready . . .

1. *You shall have no other gods before me.*
2. *You shall not make for yourself a graven image.*
3. *You shall not take the name of the LORD your God in vain.*
4. *Remember the Sabbath day, to keep it holy.*
5. *Honor your father and your mother.*
6. *You shall not murder.*
7. *You shall not commit adultery.*
8. *You shall not steal.*
9. *You shall not bear false witness against your neighbor.*
10. *You shall not covet your neighbor's house; you shall not covet your neighbor's wife, or his manservant, or his maidservant, or his ox, or his ass, or anything that is your neighbor's.*

The first four of these injunctions have nothing whatsoever to do with morality. As stated, they forbid the practice of any non–Judeo-Christian faith (like Hinduism), most religious art, utterances like "God damn it!," and all ordinary work on the Sabbath—*all under penalty of death*. We might well wonder how vital these precepts are to the maintenance of civilization.

Commandments 5 through 9 do address morality, though it is questionable how many human beings ever honored their parents or abstained from committing murder, adultery, theft, or perjury because of them. Admonishments of this kind are found in virtually every culture throughout recorded history. There is nothing especially compelling about their presentation in the Bible. There are obvious biological reasons why people tend to treat their parents well, and to think badly of murderers, adulterers, thieves, and liars. It is a scientific fact that moral emotions—like a sense of fair play or an abhorrence of cruelty—precede any exposure to scripture. Indeed, studies of primate behavior reveal that these emotions (in some form) precede humanity itself. All of our primate cousins are partial to their own kin and generally intolerant of murder and theft.

They tend not to like deception or sexual betrayal much, either. Chimpanzees, especially, display many of the complex social concerns that you would expect to see in our closest relatives in the natural world. It seems rather unlikely, therefore, that the average American will receive necessary moral instruction by seeing these precepts chiseled in marble whenever he enters a courthouse. And what are we to make of the fact that, in bringing his treatise to a close, the creator of our universe could think of no human concerns more pressing and durable than the coveting of servants and livestock?

If we are going to take the God of the Bible seriously, we should admit that He never gives us the freedom to follow the commandments we like and neglect the rest. Nor does He tell us that we can relax the penalties He has imposed for breaking them.

If you think that it would be impossible to improve upon the Ten Commandments as a statement of morality, you really owe it to yourself to read some other scriptures. Once again, we need look no further than the Jains: Mahavira, the Jain patriarch, surpassed the morality of the Bible with a single sentence: "Do not injure, abuse, oppress, enslave, insult, torment, torture, or kill any creature or living being." Imagine how different our world might be if the Bible contained this as its central precept. Christians have abused, oppressed, enslaved, insulted, tormented, tortured, and killed people in the name of God for centuries, on the basis of a theologically defensible reading of the Bible. It is impossible to behave this way by adhering to the principles of Jainism. How, then, can you argue that the Bible provides the clearest statement of morality the world has ever seen?

Real Morality

You believe that unless the Bible is accepted as the word of God, there can be no universal standard of morality. But we can easily think of objective sources of moral order that do not require the existence of a lawgiving God. For there to be objective moral truths worth knowing, there need only be better and worse ways to seek happiness in this world. If there are psychological laws that govern human well-being, knowledge of these laws would provide an enduring basis for an objective morality. While we do not have anything like a final, scientific understanding of human morality, it seems safe to say that raping and killing our neighbors is not one of its primary constituents. Everything about human experience suggests that love is more conducive to happiness than hate is. This is an *objective* claim about the human mind, about the dynamics of social relations, and about the moral order of our world. It is clearly possible to say that someone like Hitler was wrong in moral terms without reference to scripture.

While feeling love for others is surely one of the greatest sources of our own happiness, it entails a very deep concern for the happiness and suffering of those we love. Our own search for happiness, therefore, provides a rationale for self-sacrifice and self-denial. There is no question that there are times when making enormous sacrifices for the good of others is essential for one's own deeper well-being. Nothing has to be believed on insufficient evidence for people to form bonds of this sort. At various points in the Gospels, Jesus clearly tells us that love can transform human life. We need not believe that he was born of a virgin or will be returning to earth as a superhero to take these teachings to heart.

ONE OF THE most pernicious effects of religion is that it tends to divorce morality from the reality of human and animal suffering. Religion allows people to imagine that their concerns are moral when they are not—that is, when they have nothing to do with suffering or its alleviation. Indeed, religion allows people to imagine that their concerns are moral when they are highly immoral—that is, when pressing these concerns inflicts unnecessary and appalling suffering on innocent human beings. This explains why Christians like yourself expend more "moral" energy opposing abortion than fighting genocide. It explains why you are more concerned about human embryos than about the lifesaving promise of stem-cell research. And it explains why you can preach against condom use in sub-Saharan Africa while millions die from AIDS there each year.

You believe that your religious concerns

about sex, in all their tiresome immensity, have something to do with morality. And yet, your efforts to constrain the sexual behavior of consenting adults—and even to discourage your own sons and daughters from having premarital sex—are almost never geared toward the relief of human suffering. In fact, relieving suffering seems to rank rather low on your list of priorities. Your principal concern appears to be that the creator of the universe will take offense at something people do while naked. This prudery of yours contributes daily to the surplus of human misery.

Consider, for instance, the human papillomavirus (HPV). HPV is now the most common sexually transmitted disease in the United States. The virus infects over half the American population and causes nearly five thousand women to die each year from cervical cancer; the Centers for Disease Control (CDC) estimates that more than two hundred thousand die worldwide. We now have a vaccine for HPV that appears to be both safe and effective. The vaccine produced 100 percent immunity in the six thousand women who received it as part of a clinical trial. And yet, Christian conservatives in our government have resisted a vaccination program on the grounds that HPV is a valuable impediment to premarital sex. These pious men and women want to preserve cervical cancer as an incentive toward abstinence, even if it sacrifices the lives of thousands of women each year.

There is nothing wrong with encouraging teens to abstain from having sex. But we know, beyond any doubt, that teaching abstinence alone is not a good way to curb teen pregnancy or the spread of sexually transmitted disease. In fact, kids who are taught abstinence alone are less likely to use contraceptives when they do have sex, as many of them inevitably will. One study found that teen "virginity pledges" postpone intercourse for eighteen months on average—while, in the meantime, these virgin teens were more likely than their peers to engage in oral and anal sex. American teenagers engage in about as much sex as teenagers in the rest of the developed world, but American girls are four to five times more likely to become pregnant, to have a baby, or to get an abortion. Young Americans are also far more likely to be infected by HIV and other sexually transmitted diseases. The rate of gonorrhea among American teens is seventy times higher than it is among their peers in the Netherlands and France. The fact that 30 percent of our sex-education programs teach abstinence only (at a cost of more than $200 million a year) surely has something to do with this.

The problem is that Christians like yourself are not principally concerned about teen pregnancy and the spread of disease. That is, you are not worried about the *suffering* caused by sex; you are worried about sex. As if this fact needed further corroboration, Reginald Finger, an Evangelical member of the CDC's Advisory Committee on Immunization Practices, recently announced that he would consider opposing an HIV vaccine—thereby condemning millions of men and women to die unnecessarily from AIDS each year—because such a vaccine would encourage premarital sex by making it less risky. This is one of many points on which your religious beliefs become genuinely lethal.

Your qualms about embryonic stem-cell research are similarly obscene. Here are the facts: stem-cell research is one of the most promising developments in the last century of medicine. It could offer therapeutic breakthroughs for every disease or injury process that human beings suffer—for the simple reason that embryonic stem cells can become any tissue in the human body. This research may also be essential for our understanding of cancer, along with a wide variety of developmental disorders. Given these facts, it is almost impossible to exaggerate the promise of stem-cell research. It is true, of course, that research on embryonic stem cells entails the destruction of three-day-old human embryos. This is what worries you.

Let us look at the details. A three-day-old human embryo is a collection of 150 cells called a blastocyst. There are, for the sake of comparison, more than 100,000 cells in the brain of a fly. The human embryos that are destroyed in stem-cell research do not have brains, or even neurons. Consequently, there is no reason to believe they can suffer their destruction in any way at all. It is worth remembering, in this context, that when a person's brain has died, we currently deem it acceptable to harvest his organs (provided he has donated them for this purpose) and bury him in the ground. If it is acceptable to treat a person whose brain has died as something less than a human being, it should be acceptable to treat a blastocyst as such. If you are concerned about suffering in this universe, killing a fly should present you with greater moral difficulties than killing a human blastocyst.

Perhaps you think that the crucial difference between a fly and a human blastocyst is to be found in the latter's potential to become a fully developed human being. But almost every cell in your body is a potential human being, given our recent advances in genetic engineering. Every time you scratch your nose, you have committed a Holocaust of potential human beings. This is a fact. The argument from a cell's potential gets you absolutely nowhere.

But let us assume, for the moment, that every three-day-old human embryo has a soul worthy of our moral concern. Embryos at this stage occasionally split, becoming separate people (identical twins). Is this a case of one soul splitting into two? Two embryos sometimes fuse into a single individual, called a chimera. You or someone you know may have developed in this way. No doubt theologians are struggling even now to determine what becomes of the extra human soul in such a case.

Isn't it time we admitted that this arithmetic of souls does not make any sense? The naïve idea of souls in a Petri dish is intellectually indefensible. It is also *morally* indefensible, given that it now stands in the way of some of the most promising research in the history of medicine. Your beliefs about the human soul are, at this very moment, prolonging the scarcely endurable misery of tens of millions of human beings.

You believe that "life starts at the moment of conception." You believe that there are souls in each of these blastocysts and that the interests of one soul—the soul of a little girl with burns over 75 percent of her body, say—cannot trump the interests of another soul, even if that soul happens to live inside a Petri dish. Given the accommodations we have made to faith-based irrationality in our public discourse, it is often suggested, even by *advocates* of stem-cell research, that your position on this matter has some degree of moral legitimacy. It does not. Your resistance to embryonic stem-cell research is, at best, uninformed. There is, in fact, no moral reason for our federal government's unwillingness to fund this work. We should throw immense resources into stem-cell research, and we should do so immediately. Because of what Christians like yourself believe about souls, we are not doing this. In fact, several states have made such work illegal. If one experiments on a blastocyst in South Dakota, for instance, one risks spending years in prison.

The moral truth here is obvious: anyone who feels that the interests of a blastocyst just might supersede the interests of a child with a spinal cord injury has had his moral sense blinded by religious metaphysics. The link between religion and "morality"—so regularly proclaimed and so seldom demonstrated—is fully belied here, as it is wherever religious dogma supersedes moral reasoning and genuine compassion.

Doing Good for God

What about all of the good things people have done in the name of God? It is undeniable that many people of faith make heroic sacrifices to relieve the suffering of other human beings. But is it necessary to believe anything on insufficient evidence in order to behave this way? If compassion were really dependent upon religious dogmatism, how could we explain the work of secular doctors in the most war-ravaged regions of the developing world? Many doctors are moved simply to alleviate human suffering, without any thought of God. While there is no doubt that Christian missionaries are also moved by a desire to alleviate suffering, they come to the task encumbered by a dangerous and divisive mythology. Missionaries in the developing world waste a lot of time and money (not to mention the goodwill of non-Christians) proselytizing to the needy; they spread inaccurate information about contraception and sexually transmitted disease, and they withhold accurate information. While missionaries do many noble things at great risk to themselves, their dogmatism still spreads ignorance and death. By contrast, volunteers for secular organizations like Doctors Without Borders do not waste any time telling people about the virgin birth of Jesus. Nor do they tell people in sub-Saharan Africa—where nearly four million people die from AIDS every year—that condom use is sinful. Christian missionaries have been known to preach the sinfulness of condom use in villages where no other information about condoms is available. This kind of piety is genocidal.* We might also wonder, in passing, which is more moral: helping people purely out of concern for their suffering, or helping them because you think the creator of the universe will reward you for it?

---

*If you can believe it, the Vatican is currently opposed to condom use even to prevent the spread of HIV from one married partner to another. The Pope is rumored to be reconsidering this policy. Cardinal Javier Lozano Barragan, president of the Pontifical Council for Health Care, announced on Vatican radio that his office is now "conducting a very profound scientific, technical and moral study" of this issue (!). Needless to say, if Church doctrine changes as a result of these pious deliberations, it will be a sign, not that faith is wise, but that one of its dogmas has grown untenable.

Mother Teresa is a perfect example of the way in which a good person, moved to help others, can have her moral intuitions deranged by religious faith. Christopher Hitchens put it with characteristic bluntness:

> [Mother Teresa] was not a friend of the poor. She was a friend of poverty. She said that suffering was a gift from God. She spent her life opposing the only known cure for poverty, which is the empowerment of women and the emancipation of them from a livestock version of compulsory reproduction.

While I am in substantial agreement with Hitchens on this point, there is no denying that Mother Teresa was a great force for compassion. Clearly, she was moved by the suffering of her fellow human beings, and she did much to awaken others to the reality of that suffering. The problem, however, was that her compassion was channeled within the rather steep walls of her religious dogmatism. In her Nobel Prize acceptance speech, she said:

The greatest destroyer of peace is
abortion. . . . Many people are very, very
concerned with the children in India, with
the children in Africa where quite a number
die, maybe of malnutrition, of hunger and
so on, but millions are dying deliberately by
the will of the mother. And this is what is
the greatest destroyer of peace today.
Because if a mother can kill her own
child—what is left for me to kill you and
you kill me—there is nothing between.

As a diagnosis of the world's problems, these remarks are astonishingly misguided. As a statement of morality they are no better. Mother Teresa's compassion was very badly calibrated if the killing of first-trimester fetuses disturbed her more than all the other suffering she witnessed on this earth. While abortion is an ugly reality, and we should all hope for breakthroughs in contraception that reduce the need for it, one can reasonably wonder whether most aborted fetuses suffer their destruction on any level. One cannot reasonably wonder this about the millions of men, women, and children who must endure the torments of war, famine, political torture, or mental illness. At this very moment, millions of sentient people are suffering unimaginable physical and mental afflictions, in circumstances where the compassion of God is nowhere to be seen, and the compassion of human beings is often hobbled by preposterous ideas about sin and salvation. If you are worried about human suffering, abortion should rank very low on your list of concerns.

While abortion remains a ludicrously divisive issue in the United States, the "moral" position of the Church on this matter is now fully and horribly incarnated in the country of El Salvador. In El Salvador, abortion is now illegal under all circumstances. There are no exceptions for rape or incest. The moment a woman shows up at a hospital with a perforated uterus, indicating that she has had a back-alley abortion, she is shackled to her hospital bed and her body is treated as a crime scene. Forensic doctors soon arrive to examine her womb and cervix. There are women now serving prison sentences *thirty years long* for terminating their pregnancies. Imagine this, in a country that also stigmatizes the use of contraception as a sin against God. And yet this is precisely the sort of policy one would adopt if one agreed with Mother Teresa's assessment of world suffering. Indeed, the Archbishop of San Salvador actively campaigned for it. His efforts were assisted by Pope John Paul II, who declared, on a visit to Mexico City in 1999, that "the church must proclaim the Gospel of life and speak out with prophetic force against the culture of death. May the continent of hope also be the continent of life!"

Of course, the Church's position on abortion takes no more notice of the details of biology than it does of the reality of human suffering. It has been estimated that 50 percent of all human conceptions end in spontaneous abortion, usually without a woman even realizing that she was pregnant. In fact, 20 percent of all recognized pregnancies end in miscarriage. There is an obvious truth here that cries out for acknowledgment: if God exists, He is the most prolific abortionist of all.

Are Atheists Evil?

If you are right to believe that religious faith offers the only real basis for morality, then atheists should be less moral than believers. In fact, they should be utterly immoral. Are they? Do members of atheist organizations in the United States commit more than their fair share of violent crimes? Do the members of the National Academy of Sciences, 93 percent of whom do not accept the idea of God, lie and cheat and steal with abandon? We can be reasonably confident that these groups are at least as well behaved as the general population. And yet, atheists are the most reviled minority in the United States. Polls indicate that being an atheist is a perfect impediment to running for high office in our country (while being black, Muslim, or homosexual is not). Recently, crowds of thousands gathered throughout the Muslim world—burning European embassies, issuing threats, taking hostages, even killing people—in protest over twelve cartoons depicting the Prophet Muhammad that were first published in a Danish newspaper. When was the last atheist riot? Is there a newspaper anywhere on this earth that would hesitate to print cartoons about atheism for fear that its editors would be kidnapped or killed in reprisal?

Christians like yourself invariably declare

that monsters like Adolf Hitler, Joseph Stalin, Mao Zedong, Pol Pot, and Kim Il Sung spring from the womb of atheism. While it is true that such men are sometimes enemies of organized religion, they are never especially rational.* In fact, their public pronouncements are often delusional: on subjects as diverse as race, economics, national identity, the march of history, and the moral dangers of intellectu-

*And Hitler's atheism seems to have been seriously exaggerated:

> My feeling as a Christian points me to my Lord and Savior as a fighter. It points me to the man who once in loneliness, surrounded by a few followers, recognized these Jews for what they were and summoned men to fight against them and who, God's truth! was greatest not as a sufferer but as a fighter. In boundless love as a Christian and as a man I read through the passage which tells us how the Lord at last rose in His might and seized the scourge to drive out of the Temple the brood of vipers and adders. How terrific was His fight for the world against the Jewish poison. . . . as a Christian I have also a duty to my own people.

Hitler said this in a speech on April 12, 1922 (Norman H. Baynes, ed. *The Speeches of Adolf Hitler, April 1922–August 1939.* Vol. 1 of 2, pp. 19–20. Oxford University Press, 1942).

alism. The problem with such tyrants is not that they reject the dogma of religion, but that they embrace other life-destroying myths. Most become the center of a quasi-religious personality cult, requiring the continual use of propaganda for its maintenance. There is a difference between propaganda and the honest dissemination of information that we (generally) expect from a liberal democracy. Tyrants who orchestrate genocides, or who happily preside over the starvation of their own people, also tend to be profoundly idiosyncratic men, not champions of reason. Kim Il Sung, for instance, demanded that his beds at his various dwellings be situated precisely five hundred meters above sea level. His duvets had to be filled with the softest down imaginable. What is the softest down imaginable? It apparently comes from the chin of a sparrow. *Seven hundred thousand* sparrows were required to fill a single duvet. Given the profundity of his esoteric concerns, we might wonder how reasonable a man Kim Il Sung actually was.

Consider the Holocaust: the anti-Semitism that built the Nazi death camps was a direct inheritance from medieval Christianity. For centuries, Christian Europeans had viewed the Jews as the worst species of heretics and attributed every societal ill to their continued presence among the faithful. While the hatred of Jews in Germany expressed itself in a predominately secular way, its roots were religious, and the explicitly religious demonization of the Jews of Europe continued throughout the period. The Vatican itself perpetuated the blood libel in its newspapers as late as 1914.* And both Catholic and Protestant churches have a shameful record of complicity with the Nazi genocide.

Auschwitz, the Soviet gulags, and the killing fields of Cambodia are not examples of what happens to people when they become too reasonable. To the contrary, these horrors testify to the dangers of political and racial dogmatism. It is time that Christians like yourself stop pretending that a rational rejection of

---

*The "blood libel" (with respect to the Jews) consists of the false claim that Jews murder non-Jews in order to obtain their blood for use in religious rituals. This allegation is still widely believed throughout the Muslim world.

your faith entails the blind embrace of atheism as a *dogma*. One need not accept anything on insufficient evidence to find the virgin birth of Jesus to be a preposterous idea. The problem with religion—as with Nazism, Stalinism, or any other totalitarian mythology—is the problem of dogma itself. I know of no society in human history that ever suffered because its people became too desirous of evidence in support of their core beliefs.

WHILE YOU believe that bringing an end to religion is an impossible goal, it is important to realize that much of the developed world has nearly accomplished it. Norway, Iceland, Australia, Canada, Sweden, Switzerland, Belgium, Japan, the Netherlands, Denmark, and the United Kingdom are among the least religious societies on earth. According to the United Nations' Human Development Report (2005) they are also the healthiest, as indicated by life expectancy, adult literacy, per capita income, educational attainment, gender equality, homicide rate, and infant mortality. Insofar as there is a crime problem in Western Europe, it is largely the product of immigration. Seventy percent of the inmates of France's jails, for instance, are Muslim. The Muslims of Western Europe are generally not atheists. Conversely, the fifty nations now ranked lowest in terms of the United Nations' human development index are unwaveringly religious.

Other analyses paint the same picture: the United States is unique among wealthy democracies in its level of religious adherence; it is also uniquely beleaguered by high rates of homicide, abortion, teen pregnancy, sexually transmitted disease, and infant mortality. The same comparison holds true within the United States itself: Southern and Midwestern states, characterized by the highest levels of religious literalism, are especially plagued by the above indicators of societal dysfunction, while the comparatively secular states of the Northeast conform to European norms.

While political party affiliation in the United States is not a perfect indicator of religiosity, it is no secret that the "red states" are primarily red because of the overwhelming political influence of conservative Christians. If there were a strong correlation between

Christian conservatism and societal health, we might expect to see some sign of it in red-state America. We don't. Of the twenty-five cities with the lowest rates of violent crime, 62 percent are in "blue" states and 38 percent are in "red" states. Of the twenty-five most dangerous cities, 76 percent are in red states, 24 percent in blue states. In fact, three of the five most dangerous cities in the United States are in the pious state of Texas. The twelve states with the highest rates of burglary are red. Twenty-four of the twenty-nine states with the highest rates of theft are red. Of the twenty-two states with the highest rates of murder, seventeen are red.

Of course, correlational data of this sort do not resolve questions of causality—belief in God may lead to societal dysfunction; societal dysfunction may foster a belief in God; each factor may enable the other; or both may spring from some deeper source of mischief. Leaving aside the issue of cause and effect, however, these statistics prove that atheism is compatible with the basic aspirations of a civil society; they also prove, conclusively, that widespread belief in God does not ensure a society's health.

Countries with high levels of atheism are also the most charitable both in terms of the percentage of their wealth they devote to social welfare programs and the percentage they give in aid to the developing world. The dubious link between Christian literalism and Christian values is belied by other indices of social equality. Consider the ratio of salaries paid to top-tier CEOs and those paid to the same firms' average employees: in Britain it is 24:1; in France, 15:1; in Sweden, 13:1; in the United States, where 80 percent of the population expects to be called before God on Judgment Day, it is 475:1. Many a camel, it would seem, expects to pass easily through the eye of a needle.

Who Puts the Good in the "Good Book"?

Even if a belief in God had a reliable, positive effect upon human behavior, this would not offer a reason to believe in God. One can believe in God only if one thinks that God actually exists. Even if atheism led straight to moral chaos, this would not suggest that the doctrine of Christianity is *true*. Islam might be true, in that case. Or all religions might function like placebos. As descriptions of the universe, they could be utterly false but, nevertheless, useful. The evidence suggests, however, that they are both false and dangerous.

In talking about the good consequences that your beliefs have on human morality, you are following the example of religious liberals and religious moderates. Rather than say that they believe in God because certain biblical prophecies have come true, or because the miracles recounted in the Gospels are convincing, liberals and moderates tend to talk in terms of the good consequences of believing as they do. Such believers often say that they believe in God because this "gives their lives meaning." When a tsunami killed a few hundred thousand people on the day after Christmas, 2004, many conservative Christians viewed the cataclysm as evidence of God's wrath. God was apparently sending another coded message about the evils of abortion, idolatry, and homosexuality. While I consider this interpretation of events to be utterly repellent, it at least has the virtue of being reasonable, given a certain set of assumptions. Liberals and moderates, on the other

hand, refuse to draw any conclusions whatsoever about God from his works. God remains
an absolute mystery, a mere source of consolation that is compatible with the most deso-
lating evil. In the wake of the Asian tsunami,
liberals and moderates admonished one
another to look for God "not in the power that
moved the wave, but in the human response to
the wave." I think we can probably agree that
it is human benevolence on display—not
God's—whenever the bloated bodies of the
dead are dragged from the sea. On a day when
over one hundred thousand children were
simultaneously torn from their mothers' arms
and casually drowned, liberal theology must
stand revealed for what it is: the sheerest of
mortal pretenses. The theology of wrath has
far more intellectual merit. If God exists and
takes an interest in the affairs of human
beings, his will is not inscrutable. The only
thing inscrutable here is that so many otherwise rational men and women can deny the
unmitigated horror of these events and think
this the height of moral wisdom.

. . .

ALONG WITH most Christians, you believe that mortals like ourselves cannot reject the morality of the Bible. We cannot say, for instance, that God was wrong to drown most of humanity in the flood of Genesis, because this is merely the way it seems from our limited point of view. And yet, you feel that you are in a position to judge that Jesus is the Son of God, that the Golden Rule is the height of moral wisdom, and that the Bible is not itself brimming with lies. You are using your own moral intuitions to authenticate the wisdom of the Bible—and then, in the next moment, you assert that we human beings cannot possibly rely upon our own intuitions to rightly guide us in the world; rather, we must depend upon the prescriptions of the Bible. You are using your own moral intuitions to decide that the Bible is the appropriate guarantor of your moral intuitions. Your own intuitions are still primary, and your reasoning is circular.

We decide what is good in the Good Book. We read the Golden Rule and judge it to be a brilliant distillation of many of our ethical impulses. And then we come across another of God's teachings on morality: if a man discovers on his wedding night that his bride is not a virgin, he must stone her to death on her father's doorstep (Deuteronomy 22:13–21). If we are civilized, we will reject this as the vilest lunacy imaginable. Doing so requires that we exercise our own moral intuitions. The belief that the Bible is the word of God is of no help to us whatsoever.

The choice before us is simple: we can either have a twenty-first-century conversation about morality and human well-being—a conversation in which we avail ourselves of all the scientific insights and philosophical arguments that have accumulated in the last two thousand years of human discourse—or we can confine ourselves to a first-century conversation as it is preserved in the Bible. Why would anyone want to take the latter approach?

The Goodness of God

Somewhere in the world a man has abducted a little girl. Soon he will rape, torture, and kill her. If an atrocity of this kind is not occurring at precisely this moment, it will happen in a few hours, or days at most. Such is the confidence we can draw from the statistical laws that govern the lives of six billion human beings. The same statistics also suggest that this girl's parents believe—as you believe—that an all-powerful and all-loving God is watching over them and their family. Are they right to believe this? Is it *good* that they believe this?

No.

The entirety of atheism is contained in this response. Atheism is not a philosophy; it is not even a view of the world; it is simply an admission of the obvious. In fact, "atheism" is a term that should not even exist. No one ever needs to identify himself as a "non-astrologer" or a "non-alchemist." We do not have words for people who doubt that Elvis is still alive or that aliens have traversed the galaxy only to molest ranchers and their cattle. Atheism is nothing more than the noises reasonable people make in the presence of unjustified religious beliefs. An atheist is simply a person who believes that the 260 million Americans (87 percent of the population) claiming to "never doubt the existence of God" should be obliged to present evidence for his existence—and, indeed, for his

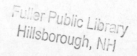

benevolence, given the relentless destruction of innocent human beings we witness in the world each day. An atheist is a person who believes that the murder of a single little girl— even once in a million years—casts doubt upon the idea of a benevolent God.

Examples of God's failure to protect humanity are everywhere to be seen. The city of New Orleans, for instance, was recently destroyed by a hurricane. More than a thousand people died; tens of thousands lost all their earthly possessions; and nearly a million were displaced. It is safe to say that almost every person living in New Orleans at the moment Hurricane Katrina struck shared your belief in an omnipotent, omniscient, and compassionate God. But what was God doing while Katrina laid waste to their city? Surely He heard the prayers of those elderly men and women who fled the rising waters for the safety of their attics, only to be slowly drowned there. These were people of faith. These were good men and women who had prayed throughout their lives. Do you have the courage to admit the obvious? These poor people died talking to an imaginary friend.

Of course, there had been ample warning that a storm "of biblical proportions" would strike New Orleans, and the human response to the ensuing disaster was tragically inept. But it was inept only by the light of *science*. Religion offered no basis for a response at all. Advance warning of Katrina's path was wrested from mute Nature by meteorological calculations and satellite imagery. God told no one of his plans. Had the residents of New Orleans been content to rely on the beneficence of God, they wouldn't have known that a killer hurricane was bearing down upon them until they felt the first gusts of wind on their faces. And yet, as will come as no surprise to you, a poll conducted by *The Washington Post* found that 80 percent of Katrina's survivors claim that the event has only strengthened their faith in God.

As Hurricane Katrina was devouring New Orleans, nearly a thousand Shiite pilgrims were trampled to death on a bridge in Iraq. These pilgrims believed mightily in the God of the Koran. Indeed, their lives were organized around the indisputable fact of his existence: their women walked veiled before Him; their men regularly murdered one another over rival interpretations of his word. It would be remarkable if a single survivor of this tragedy lost his faith. More likely, the survivors imagine that they were spared through God's grace.

It is time we recognized the boundless narcissism and self-deceit of the saved. It is time we acknowledged how disgraceful it is for the survivors of a catastrophe to believe themselves spared by a loving God, while this same God drowned infants in their cribs. Once you stop swaddling the reality of the world's suffering in religious fantasies, you will feel in your bones just how precious life is—and, indeed, how unfortunate it is that millions of human beings suffer the most harrowing abridgements of their happiness for no good reason at all.

ONE WONDERS just how vast and gratuitous a catastrophe would have to be to shake the world's faith. The Holocaust did not do it. Neither did the genocide in Rwanda, even with machete-wielding priests among the perpetrators. Five hundred million people died of smallpox in the twentieth century, many of them infants. God's ways are, indeed, inscrutable. It seems that any fact, no matter how infelicitous, can be rendered compatible with religious faith.

Of course, people of all faiths regularly assure one another that God is not responsible for human suffering. But how else can we understand the claim that God is both omniscient and omnipotent? This is the age-old problem of theodicy, of course, and we should consider it solved. If God exists, either He can do nothing to stop the most egregious calamities, or He does not care to. God, therefore, is either impotent or evil. You may now be tempted to execute the following pirouette: *God cannot be judged by human standards of morality.* But we have seen that human standards of morality are precisely what you use to establish God's goodness in the first place. And any God who could concern Himself with something as trivial as gay marriage, or the name by which He is addressed in prayer, is not as inscrutable as all that.

There is another possibility, of course, and it is both the most reasonable and least odious: the biblical God is a fiction, like Zeus and the thousands of other dead gods whom most sane human beings now ignore. Can you prove that Zeus does not exist? Of course not. And yet, just imagine if we lived in a society where people spent tens of billions of dollars of their personal income each year propitiating the gods of Mount Olympus, where the government spent billions more in tax dollars to support institutions devoted to these gods, where untold billions more in tax subsidies were given to pagan temples, where elected officials did their best to impede medical research out of deference to *The Iliad* and *The Odyssey*, and where every debate about public policy was subverted to the whims of ancient authors who wrote well, but who didn't know enough about the nature of reality to keep their excrement out of their food. This would be a horrific misappropriation of our material, moral, and intellectual resources. And yet that is exactly the society we are living in. This is the woefully irrational world that you and your fellow Christians are working so tirelessly to create.

It is terrible that we all die and lose everything we love; it is doubly terrible that so many human beings suffer needlessly while alive. That so much of this suffering can be directly attributed to religion—to religious hatreds, religious wars, religious taboos, and religious diversions of scarce resources—is what makes the honest criticism of religious faith a moral and intellectual necessity. Unfortunately, expressing such criticism places the nonbeliever at the margins of society. By merely being in touch with reality, he appears shamefully out of touch with the fantasy life of his neighbors.

The Power of Prophecy

It is often said that it is reasonable to believe that the Bible is the word of God because many of the events recounted in the New Testament confirm Old Testament prophecy. But ask yourself, how difficult would it have been for the Gospel writers to tell the story of Jesus' life so as to make it conform to Old Testament prophecy? Wouldn't it have been within the power of any mortal to write a book that confirms the predictions of a previous book? In fact, we know on the basis of textual evidence that this is what the Gospel writers did.

The writers of Luke and Matthew, for instance, declare that Mary conceived as a virgin, relying upon the Greek rendering of Isaiah 7:14. The Hebrew text of Isaiah uses the word *'almâ,* however, which simply means "young woman," without any implication of virginity. It seems all but certain that the dogma of the virgin birth, and much of the Christian world's resulting anxiety about sex, was a product of a mistranslation from the Hebrew. Another strike against the doctrine of the virgin birth is that the other evangelists have not heard of it. Mark and John both appear uncomfortable with accusations of Jesus' illegitimacy, but never mention his miraculous origins. Paul refers to Jesus as being "born of the seed of David according to the flesh" and "born of woman," without referring to Mary's virginity at all.

And the evangelists made other errors of scholarship. Matthew 27:9–10, for instance, claims to fulfill a saying that it attributes to Jeremiah. The saying actually appears in Zechariah 11:12–13. The Gospels also contradict one another outright. John tells us that Jesus was crucified the day before the Passover meal was

58

eaten; Mark says it happened the day after. In light of such discrepancies, how is it possible for you to believe that the Bible is perfect in all its parts? What do you think of Muslims, Mormons, and Sikhs who ignore similar contradictions in their holy books? They also say things like "the Holy Spirit has an eye only to substance and is not bound by words" (Luther). Does this make you even slightly more likely to accept their scriptures as the perfect word of the creator of the universe?

CHRISTIANS REGULARLY assert that the Bible predicts future historical events. For instance, Deuteronomy 28:64 says, "And the LORD will scatter you among all peoples, from one end of the earth to the other." Jesus says, in Luke 19:43–44, "For the days shall come upon you, when your enemies will cast up a bank about you and surround you, and hem you in on every side, and dash you to the ground, you and your children within you, and they will not leave one stone upon another in you; because you did not know the time of your visitation." We are meant to believe that these utterances predict the subsequent history of the Jews with such uncanny specificity so as to admit of only a supernatural explanation.

But just imagine how breathtakingly specific a work of prophecy would be, if it were actually the product of omniscience. If the Bible were such a book, it would make perfectly accurate predictions about human events. You would expect it to contain a passage such as "In the latter half of the twentieth century, humankind will develop a globally linked system of computers—the principles of which I set forth in Leviticus—and this system shall be called the Internet." The Bible contains nothing like this. In fact, it does not contain a single sentence that could not have been written by a man or woman living in the first century. This should trouble you.

A book written by an omniscient being could contain a chapter on mathematics that, after two thousand years of continuous use, would still be the richest source of mathematical insight humanity has ever known. Instead, the Bible contains no formal discussion of mathematics and some obvious mathematical errors. In two places, for instance, the Good

Book states that the ratio of the circumference of a circle to its diameter is 3:1 (I Kings 7:23–26 and II Chronicles 4:2–5). As an approximation of the constant π, this is not impressive. The decimal expansion of π runs to infinity—3.1415926535 . . .—and modern computers now allow us to calculate it to any degree of accuracy we like. But the Egyptians and Babylonians both approximated π to a few decimal places several centuries before the oldest books of the Bible were written. The Bible offers us an approximation that is terrible even by the standards of the ancient world. As should come as no surprise, the faithful have found ways of rationalizing this; but those rationalizations cannot conceal the obvious deficiency of the Bible as a source of mathematical insight. It is absolutely true to say that if the Greek mathematician Archimedes had written the relevant passages in I Kings and II Chronicles, the text would bear much greater evidence of the author's "omniscience."

Why doesn't the Bible say anything about electricity, or about DNA, or about the actual age and size of the universe? What about a cure for cancer? When we fully understand the biology of cancer, this understanding will be easily summarized in a few pages of text. Why aren't these pages, or anything remotely like them, found in the Bible? Good, pious people are dying horribly from cancer at this very moment, and many of them are children. The Bible is a very big book. God had room to instruct us in great detail about how to keep slaves and sacrifice a wide variety of animals. To one who stands outside the Christian faith, it is utterly astonishing how ordinary a book can be and still be thought the product of omniscience.

The Clash of Science and Religion

While it is now a moral necessity for scientists to speak honestly about the conflict between science and religion, even the National Academy of Sciences has declared the conflict illusory:

> At the root of the apparent conflict
> between some religions and evolution is a
> misunderstanding of the critical difference
> between religious and scientific ways of

*knowing. Religions and science answer
different questions about the world.
Whether there is a purpose to the universe
or a purpose for human existence are not
questions for science. Religious and
scientific ways of knowing have played,
and will continue to play, significant roles
in human history. . . . Science is a way of
knowing about the natural world. It is
limited to explaining the natural world
through natural causes. Science can say
nothing about the supernatural. Whether
God exists or not is a question about which
science is neutral.*

This statement is stunning for its lack of candor.
Of course, scientists live in perpetual fear of losing public funds, so the NAS may have merely
been expressing raw terror of the taxpaying
mob. The truth, however, is that the conflict
between religion and science is unavoidable.
The success of science often comes at the
expense of religious dogma; the maintenance
of religious dogma *always* comes at the expense
of science. Our religions do not simply talk
about "a purpose for human existence." Like

science, every religion makes specific claims about the way the world is. These claims purport to be about facts—the creator of the universe can hear (and will occasionally answer) your prayers; the soul enters the zygote at the moment of conception; if you do not believe the right things about God, you will suffer terribly after death. Such claims are intrinsically in conflict with the claims of science, because they are claims made on terrible evidence.

In the broadest sense, "science" (from the Latin *scire*, "to know") represents our best efforts to know what is true about our world. We need not distinguish between "hard" and "soft" science here, or between science and a branch of the humanities like history. It is a historical fact, for instance, that the Japanese bombed Pearl Harbor on December 7, 1941. Consequently, this fact forms part of the worldview of scientific rationality. Given the evidence that attests to this fact, anyone believing that it happened on another date, or that the Egyptians really dropped those bombs, has a lot of explaining to do. The core of science is not controlled experiment or mathematical modeling; it is intellectual honesty. It is time we acknowledged a basic feature of human discourse: when considering the truth of a proposition, one is either engaged in an honest appraisal of the evidence and logical arguments, or one isn't. Religion is the one area of our lives where people imagine that some other standard of intellectual integrity applies.

CONSIDER the recent deliberations of the Roman Catholic Church on the doctrine of limbo. Thirty top theologians from around the world recently met at the Vatican to discuss the question of what happens to babies who die without having undergone the sacred rite of baptism. Since the Middle Ages, Catholics have believed that such babies go to a state of limbo, where they enjoy what St. Thomas Aquinas termed "natural happiness" forever. This was in contrast to the opinion of St. Augustine, who believed that these unlucky infant souls would spend eternity in hell.

Though limbo had no real foundation in scripture, and was never official Church doctrine, it has been a major part of the Catholic tradition for centuries. In 1905, Pope Pius X appeared to fully endorse it: "Children who die without baptism go into limbo, where they do not enjoy God, but they do not suffer either." Now the great minds of the Church have convened to reconsider the matter.

Can we even conceive of a project more intellectually forlorn than this? Just imagine what these deliberations must be like. Is there the slightest possibility that someone will present evidence indicating the eternal fate of unbaptized children after death? How can any educated person think this anything but a hilarious, terrifying, and unconscionable waste of time? When one considers the fact that this is the very institution that has produced and sheltered an elite army of child-molesters, the whole enterprise begins to exude a truly diabolical aura of misspent human energy.

THE CONFLICT between science and religion is reducible to a simple fact of human cognition and discourse: either a person has good reasons for what he believes, or he does not. If there were good reasons to believe that Jesus was born of a virgin, or that Muhammad flew to heaven on a winged horse, these beliefs would necessarily form part of our rational description of the universe. Everyone recognizes that to rely upon "faith" to decide specific questions of historical fact is ridiculous—that is, until the conversation turns to the origin of books like the Bible and the Koran, to the resurrection of Jesus, to Muhammad's conversation with the archangel Gabriel, or to any other religious dogma. It is time that we admitted that faith is nothing more than the license religious people give one another to keep believing when reasons fail.

While believing strongly, without evidence, is considered a mark of madness or stupidity in any other area of our lives, faith in God still holds immense prestige in our society. Religion is the one area of our discourse where it is considered noble to pretend to be certain about things no human being could possibly be certain about. It is telling that this aura of nobility extends only to those faiths that still have many subscribers. Anyone caught worshipping Poseidon, even at sea, will be thought insane.*

The Fact of Life

All complex life on earth has developed from simpler life-forms over billions of years. This is a fact that no longer admits of intelligent dispute. If you doubt that human beings evolved from prior species, you may as well doubt that the sun is a star. Granted, the sun doesn't seem like an ordinary star, but we know that it is a star that just happens to be relatively close to the earth. Imagine your potential for embarrassment if your religious faith rested on the presumption that the sun was not a star at all. Imagine millions of Christians in the United States spending hundreds of millions of dollars each year to battle the godless astronomers and astrophysicists on this point. Imagine

---

*Truth be told, I now receive e-mails of protest from people who claim, in all apparent earnestness, to believe that Poseidon and the other gods of Greek mythology are real.

them working passionately to get their unfounded notions about the sun taught in our nation's schools. This is exactly the situation you are now in with respect to evolution.

Christians who doubt the truth of evolution are apt to say things like "Evolution is just a theory, not a fact." Such statements betray a serious misunderstanding of the way the term "theory" is used in scientific discourse. In science, facts must be explained with reference to other facts. These larger explanatory models are "theories." Theories make predictions and can, in principle, be tested. The phrase "the theory of evolution" does not in the least suggest that evolution is not a fact. One can speak about "the germ theory of disease" or "the theory of gravitation" without casting doubt upon disease or gravity as facts of nature.

It is also worth noting that one can obtain a Ph.D. in any branch of science for no other purpose than to make cynical use of scientific language in an effort to rationalize the glaring inadequacies of the Bible. A handful of Christians appear to have done this; some have even obtained their degrees from reputable universities. No doubt, others will follow in their footsteps. While such people are technically "scientists," they are not behaving like scientists. They simply are not engaged in an honest inquiry into the nature of the universe. And their proclamations about God and the failures of Darwinism do not in the least signify that there is a legitimate scientific controversy about evolution. In 2005, a survey was conducted in thirty-four countries measuring the percentage of adults who accept evolution. The United States ranked thirty-third, just above Turkey. Meanwhile, high school students in the United States test below those of every European and Asian nation in their understanding of science and math. These data are unequivocal: we are building a civilization of ignorance.

Here is what we know. We know that the universe is far older than the Bible suggests. We know that all complex organisms on earth, including ourselves, evolved from earlier organisms over the course of billions of years. The evidence for this is utterly overwhelming. There is no question that the diverse life we see around us is the expression of a genetic code written in the molecule DNA, that DNA undergoes chance mutations, and that some mutations increase an organism's odds of surviving and reproducing in a given environment. This process of mutation and natural selection has allowed isolated populations of individuals to interbreed and, over vast stretches of time, form new species. There is no question that human beings evolved from nonhuman ancestors in this way. We know, from genetic evidence, that we share an ancestor with apes and monkeys, and that this ancestor in turn shared an ancestor with the bats and the flying lemurs. There is a widely branching tree of life whose basic shape and character is now very well understood. Consequently, there is no reason whatsoever to believe that individual species were created in their present forms. How the process of evolution got started is still a mystery, but that does not in the least suggest that a deity is likely to be lurking at the bottom of it all. Any honest reading of the biblical account of creation suggests that God created all animals and plants as we now see them. There is no question that the Bible is wrong about this.

Many Christians who want to cast doubt upon the truth of evolution now advocate something called intelligent design (ID). The problem with ID is that it is nothing more than a program of political and religious advocacy masquerading as science. Since a belief in the biblical God finds no support in our growing scientific understanding of the world, ID theorists invariably stake their claim on the areas of scientific ignorance.

The argument for ID has proceeded on many fronts at once. Like countless theists before them, fanciers of ID regularly argue that the very fact that the universe exists proves the existence of God. The argument runs more or less like this: everything that exists has a cause; space and time exist; space and time must, therefore, have been caused by something that stands outside of space and time; and the only thing that transcends space and time, and yet retains the power to create, is God. Many Christians like yourself find this argument compelling. And yet, even if we granted its primary claims (each of which requires much more discussion than ID theorists ever acknowledge), the final conclusion does not follow. Who is to say that the only thing that could give rise to space and time is a supreme being? Even if we accepted that our universe simply had to be designed by a designer, this would not suggest that this designer is the biblical God, or that He approves of Christianity. If intelligently designed, our universe could be running as a simulation on an alien supercomputer. Or it could be the work of an evil God, or of two such gods playing tug-of-war with a larger cosmos.

As many critics of religion have pointed out, the notion of a creator poses an immediate problem of an infinite regress. If God created the universe, what created God? To say that God, by definition, is uncreated simply begs the question. Any being capable of creating a complex world promises to be very complex himself. As the biologist Richard Dawkins has observed repeatedly, the only natural process we know of that could produce a being capable of designing things is evolution.

The truth is that no one knows how or why the universe came into being. It is not clear that we can even speak coherently about the creation of the universe, given that such an event can be conceived only with reference to time, and here we are talking about the birth of space-time itself.* Any intellectually honest person will admit that he *does not know* why the universe exists. Scientists, of course, readily admit their ignorance on this point. Religious believers do not. One of the monumental ironies of religious discourse can be appreciated in the frequency with which people of faith praise themselves for their humility, while condemning scientists and other non-believers for their intellectual arrogance. There is, in fact, no worldview more reprehensible in its arrogance than that of a religious believer: *the creator of the universe takes an interest in me, approves of me, loves me, and will reward me after death; my current beliefs, drawn from scripture, will remain the best statement of the truth until the end of the world; everyone who disagrees with me will spend eternity in hell.* . . . An average Christian, in an average church, listening to an average Sunday sermon has achieved a level of arrogance simply

*The physicist Stephen Hawking, for instance, pictures space-time as a four-dimensional, closed manifold, without beginning or end (much like the surface of a sphere).

unimaginable in scientific discourse—and there have been some extraordinarily arrogant scientists.

OVER 99 PERCENT of the species that ever walked, flew, or slithered upon this earth are now extinct. This fact alone appears to rule out intelligent design. When we look at the natural world, we see extraordinary complexity, but we do not see optimal design. We see redundancy, regressions, and unnecessary complications; we see bewildering inefficiencies that result in suffering and death. We see flightless birds and snakes with pelvises. We see species of fish, salamanders, and crustaceans that have nonfunctional eyes, because they continued to evolve in darkness for millions of years. We see whales that produce teeth during fetal development, only to reabsorb them as adults. Such features of our world are utterly mysterious if God created all species of life on earth "intelligently"; none of them are perplexing in light of evolution.

The biologist J. B. S. Haldane is reported to have said that, if there is a God, He has "an inordinate fondness for beetles." One would have hoped that an observation this devastating would have closed the book on creationism for all time. The truth is that, while there are now around three hundred and fifty thousand known species of beetles, God appears to have an even greater fondness for viruses. Biologists estimate that there are at least ten strains of virus for every species of animal on earth. Many viruses are benign, of course, and some ancient virus may have played an important role in the emergence of complex organisms. But viruses tend to use organisms like you and me as their borrowed genitalia. Many of them invade our cells only to destroy them, destroying us in the process—horribly, mercilessly, relentlessly. Viruses like HIV, as well as a wide range of harmful bacteria, can be seen evolving right under our noses, developing resistance to antiviral and antibiotic drugs to the detriment of everyone. Evolution both predicts and explains this phenomenon; the book of Genesis does not. How can you imagine that religious faith offers the best account of these realities, or that they suggest some deeper, compassionate purpose of an omniscient being?

Our own bodies testify to the whimsy and incompetence of the creator. As embryos, we produce tails, gill sacs, and a full coat of apelike hair. Happily, most of us lose these charming accessories before birth. This bizarre sequence of morphology is readily interpreted in evolutionary and genetic terms; it is an utter mystery if we are the products of intelligent design. Men have a urinary tract that runs directly through the prostate gland. The prostate tends to swell throughout life. Consequently, most men over the age of sixty can testify that at least one design on God's green earth leaves much to be desired. A woman's pelvis has not been as intelligently designed as it could have been to assist in the miracle of birth. Consequently, each year hundreds of thousands of women suffer prolonged and obstructed labor that results in a rupture known as an obstetric fistula. Women in the developing world who suffer this condition become incontinent and are often abandoned by their husbands and exiled from their communities. The United Nations

Population Fund estimates that more than two million women live with fistula today.*

Examples of unintelligent design in nature are so numerous that an entire book could be written simply listing them. I will permit myself just one more example. The human respiratory and digestive tracts share a little plumbing at the pharynx. In the United States alone, this intelligent design feature lands tens of thousands of children in the emergency room each year. Some hundreds choke to death. Many others suffer irreparable brain injury. What compassionate purpose does this serve? Of course,

---

*The cure for obstetric fistula is, as it turns out, a simple surgical procedure—not prayer. While many people of faith seem convinced that prayer can heal a wide variety of illnesses (despite what the best scientific research indicates), it is curious that prayer is only ever believed to work for illnesses and injuries that can be self-limiting. No one, for instance, ever seriously expects that prayer will cause an amputee to regrow a missing limb. Why not? Salamanders manage this routinely, presumably without prayer. If God answers prayers—*ever*—why wouldn't He occasionally heal a deserving amputee? And why wouldn't people of faith expect prayer to work in such cases? There is a very clever Web site devoted to exploring this very mystery: www.whydoesgodhateamputees.com.

we can *imagine* a compassionate purpose: perhaps the parents of these children needed to be taught a lesson; perhaps God has prepared a special reward in heaven for every child who chokes to death on a bottle cap. The problem, however, is that such imaginings are compatible with *any* state of the world. What horrendous mishap could not be rationalized in this way? And why would you be inclined to think like this? How is it *moral* to think like this?

Religion, Violence, and the Future of Civilization

Billions of people share your belief that the creator of the universe wrote (or dictated) one of our books. Unfortunately, there are many books that pretend to divine authorship, and they make incompatible claims about how we all must live. Competing religious doctrines have shattered our world into separate moral communities, and these divisions have become a continual source of human conflict.

In response to this situation, many sensible people advocate something called religious tolerance. While religious tolerance is surely better than religious war, tolerance is not without its problems. Our fear of provoking religious hatred has rendered us unwilling to criticize ideas that are increasingly maladaptive and patently ridiculous. It has also obliged us to lie to ourselves—repeatedly and at the highest levels of discourse—about the compatibility between religious faith and scientific rationality. Our competing religious certainties are impeding the emergence of a viable, global civilization. Religious faith—faith that there is a God who cares what name He is called, faith that Jesus is coming back to earth, faith that Muslim martyrs go straight to Paradise—is on the wrong side of an escalating war of ideas.

Religion raises the stakes of human conflict much higher than tribalism, racism, or politics ever can, as it is the only form of in-group/out-group thinking that casts the differences between people in terms of eternal rewards and punishments. One of the enduring pathologies of human culture is the tendency to raise children to fear and demonize other human beings on the basis of religious faith. Consequently, faith inspires violence in at least two ways. First, people often kill other human beings because they believe that the creator of the universe wants them to do it. Islamist terrorism is a recent example of this sort of behavior. Second, far greater numbers of people fall into conflict with one another because they define their moral community on the basis of their religious affiliation: Muslims side with other Muslims, Protestants with Protestants, Catholics with Catholics. These conflicts are not always explicitly religious. But the bigotry and hatred that divide one community from another are often the products of their religious identities. Conflicts that seem driven entirely by terrestrial concerns, therefore, are often deeply rooted in religion. The fighting that has plagued Palestine (Jews vs. Muslims), the Balkans (Orthodox Serbians vs. Catholic Croatians; Orthodox Serbians vs. Bosnian and Albanian Muslims), Northern Ireland (Protestants vs. Catholics), Kashmir (Muslims vs. Hindus), Sudan (Muslims vs. Christians and animists),* Nigeria (Muslims vs. Christians), Ethiopia and Eritrea

*This long-standing civil war is distinct from the genocide that is currently occurring in the Darfur region of Sudan.

(Muslims vs. Christians), Ivory Coast (Muslims vs. Christians), Sri Lanka (Sinhalese Buddhists vs. Tamil Hindus), Philippines (Muslims vs. Christians), Iran and Iraq (Shiite vs. Sunni Muslims), and the Caucasus (Orthodox Russians vs. Chechen Muslims; Muslim Azerbaijanis vs. Catholic and Orthodox Armenians) are merely a few, recent cases in point.

And yet, while the religious divisions in our world are self-evident, many people still imagine that religious conflict is always caused by a lack of education, by poverty, or by politics. Most nonbelievers, liberals, and moderates apparently think that no one ever really sacrifices his life, or the lives of others, on account of his religious beliefs. Such people simply do not know what it is like to be certain of Paradise. Consequently, they can't believe that anyone *is* certain of Paradise. It is worth remembering that the September 11 hijackers were college-educated, middle-class people who had no discernible experience of political oppression. They did, however, spend a remarkable amount of time at their local mosque talking about the depravity of infidels and about the pleasures that await martyrs in Paradise. How many more architects and engineers must hit the wall at four hundred miles an hour before we admit to ourselves that jihadist violence is not merely a matter of education, poverty, or politics? The truth, astonishingly enough, is this: in the year 2006, a person can have sufficient intellectual and material resources to build a nuclear bomb and still believe that he will get seventy-two virgins in Paradise. Western secularists, liberals, and moderates have been very slow to understand this. The cause of their confusion is simple: they don't know what it is like to *really* believe in God.

LET US BRIEFLY consider where our discordant religious certainties are leading us on a global scale. The earth is now home to about 1.4 billion Muslims, many of whom believe that one day you and I will either convert to Islam, live in subjugation to a Muslim caliphate, or be put to death for our unbelief. Islam is now the fastest-growing religion in Europe. The birthrate among European Muslims is three times that of their non-Muslim neighbors. If current trends continue, France will be a majority-

Muslim country in twenty-five years—and that is if immigration were to stop tomorrow. Throughout Europe, Muslim communities often show little inclination to acquire the secular and civil values of their host countries, and yet they exploit these values to the utmost, demanding tolerance for their misogyny, their anti-Semitism, and the religious hatred that is regularly preached in their mosques. Forced marriages, honor killings, punitive gang rapes, and a homicidal loathing of homosexuals are now features of an otherwise secular Europe, courtesy of Islam.* Political correctness and

*Women are thought to "dishonor" their families by refusing to enter into an arranged marriage, seeking a divorce, committing adultery, and even by being raped or suffering some other form of sexual assault. Women in these situations are often murdered by their fathers, husbands, or brothers, sometimes with the collaboration of other women. Honor killing is, perhaps, best viewed as a cultural (rather than strictly religious) phenomenon, and it is not unique to the Muslim world. The practice, however, finds considerable support under Islam, given that the religion explicitly views women as the property of men and considers adultery a capital offense. Throughout the Muslim world, a woman who reports being raped runs the risk of being murdered as an "adulteress": she has, after all, admitted to having sex outside of marriage.

the fear of racism have made many Europeans reluctant to oppose the terrifying religious commitments of the extremists in their midst. With a few exceptions, the only public figures who have had the courage to speak honestly about the threat that Islam now poses to European society seem to be fascists. This does not bode well for the future of civilization.

The idea that Islam is a "peaceful religion hijacked by extremists" is a fantasy, and it is now a particularly dangerous fantasy for Muslims to indulge. It is not at all clear how we should proceed in our dialogue with the Muslim world, but deluding ourselves with euphemisms is not the answer. It is now a truism in foreign policy circles that real reform in the Muslim world cannot be imposed from the outside. But it is important to recognize why this is so—it is so because most Muslims are *utterly deranged by their religious faith.* Muslims tend to view questions of public policy and global conflict in terms of their affiliation with Islam. And Muslims who don't view the world in these terms risk being branded as apostates and killed by other Muslims.

But how can we ever hope to reason with the Muslim world if we are not reasonable ourselves? It accomplishes nothing to merely declare that "we all worship the same God." We do not all worship the same God, and nothing attests to this fact more eloquently than our history of religious bloodshed. Within Islam, the Shi'a and the Sunni can't even agree to worship the same God in the same way, and over this they have been killing one another for centuries.

It seems profoundly unlikely that we will heal the divisions in our world through interfaith dialogue. Devout Muslims are as convinced as you are that their religion is perfect and that any deviation leads directly to hell. It is easy, of course, for the representatives of the major religions to occasionally meet and agree that there should be peace on earth, or that compassion is the common thread that unites all the world's faiths. But there is no escaping the fact that a person's religious beliefs uniquely determine what he thinks peace is good for, as well as what he means by a term like "compassion." There are millions—maybe hundreds of millions—of Muslims who would be willing to die before they would allow your version of compassion to gain a foothold on the Arabian Peninsula. How can interfaith dialogue, even at the highest level, reconcile worldviews that are fundamentally incompatible and, in principle, immune to revision? The truth is, it really matters what billions of human beings believe and why they believe it.

Conclusion

One of the greatest challenges facing civilization in the twenty-first century is for human beings to learn to speak about their deepest personal concerns—about ethics, spiritual experience, and the inevitability of human suffering—in ways that are not flagrantly irrational. We desperately need a public discourse that encourages critical thinking and intellectual honesty. Nothing stands in the way of this project more than the respect we accord religious faith.

I would be the first to admit that the prospects for eradicating religion in our time do not seem good. Still, the same could have been said about efforts to abolish slavery at the end of the eighteenth century. Anyone who spoke with confidence about eradicating slavery in the United States in the year 1775 surely appeared to be wasting his time, and wasting it dangerously.

The analogy is not perfect, but it is suggestive. If we ever do transcend our religious bewilderment, we will look back upon this period in human history with horror and amazement. How could it have been possible for people to believe such things in the twenty-first century? How could it be that they allowed their societies to become so dangerously fragmented by empty notions about God and Paradise? The truth is, some of your most cherished beliefs are as embarrassing as those that sent the last slave ship sailing to America as late as 1859 (the same year that Darwin published *The Origin of Species*).

Clearly, it is time we learned to meet our emotional needs without embracing the preposterous. We must find ways to invoke the power of ritual and to mark those transitions in every human life that demand profundity—birth, marriage, death—without lying to ourselves about the nature of reality. Only then will the practice of raising our children to believe that they are Christian, Muslim, or Jewish be widely recognized as the ludicrous obscenity that it is. And only then will we stand a chance of healing the deepest and most dangerous fractures in our world.

. . .

I HAVE NO doubt that your acceptance of Christ
coincided with some very positive changes in
your life. Perhaps you now love other people in
a way that you never imagined possible. You
may even experience feelings of bliss while
praying. I do not wish to denigrate any of these
experiences. I would point out, however, that
billions of other human beings, in every time
and place, have had similar experiences—but
they had them while thinking about Krishna,
or Allah, or the Buddha, while making art
or music, or while contemplating the beauty of
Nature. There is no question that it is possible
for people to have profoundly transformative
experiences. And there is no question that it is
possible for them to misinterpret these experiences, and to further delude themselves about
the nature of reality. You are, of course, right to
believe that there is more to life than simply
understanding the structure and contents of
the universe. But this does not make unjustified (and unjustifiable) claims about its structure and contents any more respectable.

It is important to realize that the distinction

between science and religion is not a matter of excluding our ethical intuitions and spiritual experiences from our conversation about the world; it is a matter of our being honest about what we can reasonably conclude on their basis. There are good reasons to believe that people like Jesus and the Buddha weren't talking nonsense when they spoke about our capacity as human beings to transform our lives in rare and beautiful ways. But any genuine exploration of ethics or the contemplative life demands the same standards of reasonableness and self-criticism that animate all intellectual discourse.

As a biological phenomenon, religion is the product of cognitive processes that have deep roots in our evolutionary past. Some researchers have speculated that religion itself may have played an important role in getting large groups of prehistoric humans to socially cohere. If this is true, we can say that religion has served an important purpose. This does not suggest, however, that it serves an important purpose *now*. There is, after all, nothing more natural than rape. But no one would argue that rape is good, or compatible with a civil society, because it may have had evolutionary advantages for our ancestors. That religion may have served some necessary function for us in the past does not preclude the possibility that it is now the greatest impediment to our building a global civilization.

THIS LETTER is the product of failure—the failure of the many brilliant attacks upon religion that preceded it, the failure of our schools to announce the death of God in a way that each generation can understand, the failure of the media to criticize the abject religious certainties of our public figures—failures great and small that have kept almost every society on this earth muddling over God and despising those who muddle differently.

Nonbelievers like myself stand beside you, dumbstruck by the Muslim hordes who chant death to whole nations of the living. But we stand dumbstruck by *you* as well—by your denial of tangible reality, by the suffering you create in service to your religious myths, and by your attachment to an imaginary God. This letter has been an expression of that amazement—and, perhaps, of a little hope.

AFTERWORD TO THE
VINTAGE BOOKS EDITION

Humanity has had a long fascination with blood sacrifice. In fact, it has been by no means uncommon for a child to be born into this world only to be patiently and lovingly reared by religious maniacs, who believe that the best way to keep the sun on its course or to ensure a rich harvest is to lead him by tender hand into a field or to a mountaintop and bury, butcher, or burn him alive as an offering to an invisible God. Countless children have been unlucky enough to be born in so dark an age, when ignorance and fantasy were indistinguishable from knowledge and where the drumbeat of religious fanaticism kept perfect time with every human heart. In fact, almost no culture has been exempt from this evil: the Sumerians, Phoenicians, Egyptians, Hebrews, Canaanites, Maya,

Inca, Aztecs, Olmecs, Greeks, Romans, Carthaginians, Teutons, Celts, Druids, Vikings, Gauls, Hindus, Thais, Chinese, Japanese, Maoris, Melanesians, Tahitians, Hawaiians, Balinese, Australian aborigines, Iroquois, Huron, Cherokee, and innumerable other societies ritually murdered their fellow human beings because they believed that invisible gods and goddesses, having an appetite for human flesh, could be so propitiated. Many of their victims were of the same opinion, in fact, and went willingly to slaughter, fully convinced that their deaths would transform the weather, or cure the king of his venereal disease, or in some other way spare their fellows the wrath of the Unseen.

In many societies, whenever a new building was constructed, it was thought only prudent to pacify the local deities by burying children alive beneath its foundations (this is how faith sometimes operates in a world without structural engineers). Many societies regularly sacrificed virgins to ward off floods. Others killed their firstborn children, and even ate them, as a way of ensuring a mother's ongoing fertility. In India, living infants were ritually fed to sharks at the mouth of the Ganges for the same purpose. Indians also burned widows alive so that they could follow their husbands into the next world. Leaving nothing to chance, Indians also sowed their fields with the flesh of a certain caste of men, raised especially for this purpose and dismembered while alive, to ensure that every crop of tumeric would be appropriately crimson. The British were actually hard-pressed to put an end to these pious atrocities.

In some cultures whenever a nobleman died, other men and women allowed themselves to be buried alive so as to serve as his retainers in the next world. In ancient Rome, children were occasionally slaughtered so that the future could be read in their entrails. Some Fijian prodigy devised a powerful sacrament called "Vakatoga," which required that a victim's limbs be cut off and eaten while he watched. Among the Iroquois, prisoners taken captive in war were often permitted to live among the tribe for many years, and even to marry, all the while being doomed to be flayed alive as an oblation to the God of War; whatever children they produced while in captivity were disposed of in the same ritual. Certain

African tribes have a long history of murdering people to send as couriers in a one-way dialogue with their ancestors or to convert their body parts into magical charms. Ritual murders of this sort continue in many African societies to this day.*

It is essential to realize that such obscene misuses of human life have always been explicitly religious. They are the product of what people think they know about invisible gods and goddesses, and of what they manifestly do *not* know about biology, meteorology, medicine, physics, and a dozen other specific sciences. And it is astride this contemptible history of religious atrocity and scientific ignorance that Christianity now stands as an absurdly unselfconscious apotheosis. The notion that Jesus Christ died for our sins and that his death constitutes a successful propitiation of a "loving" God is a direct and undisguised inheritance of the superstitious bloodletting that has plagued bewildered people throughout history.

*For more on the history of human sacrifice see N. Davies, *Human Sacrifice: In History and Today*. Dorset.

Of course, the God of Abraham was no stranger to ritual murder. Occasionally, He condemns the practice (Deuteronomy 12:31; Jeremiah 19:4–5; Ezekiel 16:20–21); at other points, He requires or rewards it (Exodus 22:29–30; Judges 11:29–40; 1 Kings 13:1–2; 2 Kings 3:27; 2 Kings 23:20–25; Numbers 31:40; Deuteronomy 13:13–19). In the case of Abraham, God demands that he sacrifice his son Isaac but then stays his hand at the last moment (Genesis 22:1–18), without ever suggesting that the act of slaughtering one's own child is immoral. Elsewhere, God confesses to inspiring child sacrifice so as to defile its practitioners (Ezekiel 20:26), while getting into the act Himself by slaying the firstborn of Egypt (Exodus 11:5). The rite of circumcision emerges as a surrogate for child sacrifice (Exodus 4:24–26), and God seems to generally encourage the substitution of animals for people. Indeed, His thirst for the blood of animals, as well as His attentiveness to the niceties of their slaughter and holocaust, is almost impossible to exaggerate.

Upon seeing Jesus for the first time, John the Baptist is rumored to have said, "Behold the Lamb of God, which taketh away the sin of the world" (John 1:29). For most Christians, this bizarre opinion still stands, and it remains the core of their faith. Christianity is more or less synonymous with the proposition that the crucifixion of Jesus represents a final, sufficient offering of blood to a God who absolutely requires it (Hebrews 9:22–28). Christianity amounts to the claim that we must love and be loved by a God who approves of the scapegoating, torture, and murder of one man—his son, incidentally—in compensation for the misbehavior and thought-crimes of all others.

Let the good news go forth: we live in a cosmos, the vastness of which we can scarcely even indicate in our thoughts, on a planet teeming with creatures we have only begun to understand, but the whole project was actually brought to a glorious fulfillment over twenty centuries ago, after one species of primate (our own) climbed down out of the trees, invented agriculture and iron tools, glimpsed (as through a glass, darkly) the possibility of keeping its excrement out of its food, and then singled out one among its number to be viciously flogged and nailed to a cross.

Add to this abject mythology surrounding one man's death by torture—Christ's passion—

the symbolic cannibalism of the Eucharist. Did I say "symbolic"? Sorry, according to the Vatican it is most assuredly not symbolic. In fact, the judgment of the Council of Trent remains in effect:

> *I likewise profess that in the Mass a true, proper and propitiatory sacrifice is offered to God on behalf of the living and the dead, and that the body and blood together with the soul and divinity of our Lord Jesus Christ is truly, really, and substantially present in the most holy sacrament of the Eucharist, and that there is a change of the whole substance of the bread into the body, and of the whole substance of the wine into blood; and this change the Catholic Church calls transubstantiation. I also profess that the whole and entire Christ and a true sacrament is received under each separate species.*

Of course, Catholics have done some very strenuous and unconvincing theology in this area, in an effort to make sense of how they can really eat the body of Jesus, not mere crackers enrobed in metaphor, and really drink his blood without, in fact, being a cult of crazy cannibals. Suffice it to say, however, that a worldview in which "propitiatory sacrifices on behalf of the living and the dead" figure prominently is rather difficult to defend in the year 2007. But this has not stopped otherwise intelligent and well-intentioned people from defending it.

And now we learn that even Mother Teresa, the most celebrated exponent of this dogmatism in a century, had her doubts all the while—about the presence of Christ in the Eucharist, about heaven, and even about the existence of God:

> *Lord, my God, who am I that You should forsake me? The Child of your Love—and now become as the most hated one—the one—You have thrown away as unwanted—unloved. I call, I cling, I want—and there is no One to answer—no One on Whom I can cling—no, No One.—Alone . . . Where is my Faith— even deep down right in there is nothing, but emptiness & darkness—My God—*

how painful is this unknown pain—I have
no Faith—I dare not utter the words &
thoughts that crowd in my heart—& make
me suffer untold agony.

So many unanswered questions live
within me afraid to uncover them—
because of the blasphemy—If there be
God—please forgive me—When I try to
raise my thoughts to Heaven—there is
such convicting emptiness that those very
thoughts return like sharp knives & hurt
my very soul.—I am told God loves me—
and yet the reality of darkness & coldness
& emptiness is so great that nothing
touches my soul. Did I make a mistake in
surrendering blindly to the Call of the
Sacred Heart?

—addressed to Jesus, at the
suggestion of a confessor, undated

Mother Teresa's recently published letters reveal
a mind riven by doubt (and well it should
have been). They also reveal a woman who was
surely suffering from run-of-the-mill depres-
sion, though even secular commentators have
begun to politely dress this fact in the colors

of the saints and martyrs. Mother Teresa's response to her own bewilderment and hypocrisy (her term) reveals just how like quicksand religious faith can be. Her doubts about God's existence were interpreted by her confessor as a sign that she was now sharing Christ's torment upon the cross; this exaltation of her wavering faith allowed her "to love the darkness" she experienced in God's apparent absence. Such is the genius of the unfalsifiable. We can see the same principle at work among her fellow Catholics: Mother Teresa's doubts have only enhanced her stature in the eyes of the Church, being interpreted as a further confirmation of God's grace. Ask yourself, when even the doubts of experts are taken to confirm a doctrine, what could possibly disconfirm it?

It has been more than a year since *Letter to a Christian Nation* was published, and the book has continued to draw steady fire. Much of the criticism leveled at it has been bundled with attacks upon my first book, *The End of Faith*, and upon other atheist bestsellers: especially Dan Dennett's *Breaking the Spell*, Richard Dawkins's *The God Delusion*, and Christopher Hitchens's *God Is Not Great*. In fact, Dennett,

Dawkins, Hitchens, and I have been regularly assailed as though we were a single person with four heads. The accusations and arguments against us are always the same, and they always miss the point. Indeed, what is most surprising about debating the faithful is how few surprises there are.

The Problem with Moderate Religion

Whenever nonbelievers like myself criticize Christians for believing in the imminent return of Christ, or Muslims for believing in martyrdom, religious moderates declare that we have caricatured Christianity and Islam, taken "extremists" to be representative of these "great" religions, or otherwise overlooked a shimmering ocean of nuance. We are invariably told that a mature understanding of scripture renders faith perfectly compatible with reason, and that our attacks upon religion are, therefore, "simplistic," "dogmatic," or even "fundamentalist."

But there are several problems with such a defense of religion. First, many moderates (and even some secularists) assume that religious "extremism" is rare and therefore not all that consequential. But religious extremism is not rare, and it is hugely consequential. The United States is now a nation of 300 million souls, wielding more influence than any people in human history, and yet 240 million of these souls apparently believe that Jesus will return someday and orchestrate the end of the world with his magic powers. This hankering for a denominational, spiritual oblivion is extreme in almost every sense—it is extremely silly, extremely dangerous, extremely worthy of denigration—but it is not extreme in the sense of being rare. Of course, moderates may wonder whether as many people believe such things as say they do. In fact, many atheists are confident that our opinion polls are out of register with what people actually think in the privacy of their own minds. But there is no question that most Americans reliably *claim* to believe the preposterous, and these claims themselves have done genuine harm to our political discourse, to our public policy, and to our reputation in the world.

Religious moderates also tend to imagine that there is some bright line of separation between extremist and moderate religion. But there isn't. Scripture itself remains a perpetual engine of extremism: because, while He may be many things, the God of the Bible and the Qur'an is not a moderate. Reading scripture more closely, one does not find reasons to be a religious moderate; one finds reasons to be a proper religious lunatic—to fear the fires of hell, to despise nonbelievers, to persecute homosexuals, etc. Of course, anyone can cherry-pick scripture and find reasons to love his neighbor and to turn the other cheek. But the more fully a person grants credence to these books, the more he will be convinced that infidels, heretics, and apostates deserve to be smashed to atoms in God's loving machinery of justice.

Religious moderates invariably claim to be more "sophisticated" than religious fundamentalists (and atheists). But how does one become a sophisticated believer? By acknowledging just how dubious many of the claims of scripture are, and thereafter reading it selectively, bowdlerizing it if need be, and allowing its assertions about reality to be continually trumped by fresh insights—scientific ("You mean the world isn't 6,000 years old? Okay."),

medical ("I should take my daughter to a neu-
rologist and not to an exorcist? Seems reasonable . . ."), and moral ("I can't beat my slaves? I
can't even *keep* slaves? Hmm . . ."). There is a
pattern here, and it is undeniable. Religious
moderation is the direct result of taking scripture less and less seriously. So why not take it
less seriously still? Why not admit that the
Bible is merely a collection of imperfect books
written by highly fallible human beings?

Another problem with religious moderation
is that it represents precisely the sort of thinking
that will prevent a rational and nondenomina-
tional spirituality from ever emerging in our
world. Whatever is true about us, spiritually
and ethically, must be discoverable *now*. Consequently, it makes no sense at all to have one's
spiritual life pegged to rumors of ancient miracles. What we need is a discourse about ethics
and spiritual experience that is as uncon-
strained by ancient ignorance as the discourse
of science already is. Science really does transcend the vagaries of culture: there is no such
thing as "Japanese" as opposed to "French" science; we don't speak of "Hindu biology" and
"Jewish chemistry." Imagine a world in which

we could have a truly honest and open-ended conversation about our place in the universe and about the possibilities of deepening our self-understanding, ethical wisdom, and compassion. By living as if some measure of sectarian superstition were essential for human happiness, religious moderates prevent such a conversation from ever taking shape.

Intellectual Honesty

Religion once offered answers to many questions that have now been ceded to the care of science. This process of scientific conquest and religious forfeiture has been relentless, one directional, and utterly predictable. As it turns out, real knowledge, being both valid and verifiable across cultures, is the only remedy for religious discord. Muslims and Christians cannot disagree about the causes of cholera, for instance, because whatever their traditions might say about infectious disease, a genuine understanding of cholera has arrived from another quarter. Epidemiology trumps religious superstition (eventually), especially when people are watching their children die. This is where our hope for a truly nonsectarian future lies: when things matter, people tend to want to understand what is actually going on in the world. Science delivers this understanding in torrents; it also offers an honest appraisal of its current limitations. Religion fails on both counts.

Hoping to reconcile their faith with our growing scientific understanding of the world, many believers have taken refuge in Stephen J. Gould's quisling formulation of "nonoverlapping magisteria"—the idea that science and religion, properly construed, cannot be in conflict, because they represent different domains of expertise. Let's see how this works: while science is the best authority on the workings of physical universe, religion is the best authority on . . . what exactly? The *non*-physical universe? Probably not. What about meaning, values, ethics, and the good life? Unfortunately, most people—even most scientists and secularists—have ceded these essential components of human happiness to the care of theologians and religious apologists without argument. This has kept religion in good standing even while its authority has been battered and nullified on every other front.

But what special competence does a priest, rabbi, or imam have to judge the ethical implications of embryonic stem-cell research, family planning, or preventative war? The truth is that a person's knowledge of a scriptural tradition is no more relevant to ethics than it is to astronomy. Representatives of the world's religions can tell us what their congregations *believe* on a wide variety of issues (and believe, generally, on bad evidence); they can tell us what their holy books say one *ought* to believe to escape the fires of hell; but what they cannot do—or can do no better than butchers, bakers, and candlestick makers—is offer an account of why these orthodox positions are *ethical*. Is it ethical to kill a person for changing his religion? I'd stake my life that the answer is "no." But, according to a recent poll, 36 percent of British Muslims (ages 16–24) disagree with me.* As it turns out, they are on firm ground theologically: for while the Qur'an does not explicitly demand the murder of apostates, the sacred literature of the *hadith*

---

*"Multiculturalism 'drives young Muslims to shun British values.' " *Daily Mail* (January 29, 2007).

does, repeatedly and without equivocation. Is this edict ethical? Is it compatible with civil society? Is the reliance upon authority that has delivered this barbarism down through the generations even remotely compatible with science?

It is, of course, trivially true to say that religion and science are compatible because some scientists are (or claim to be) religious. But this is like saying that science and ignorance are compatible because many scientists freely admit their ignorance on a wide range of topics. To clarify these issues, it is helpful to remind ourselves that both religion and science are constituted by beliefs and their justification, or lack thereof. Is there a conflict between justified and unjustified belief? Of course, and it is zero-sum. Given that faith is generally nothing more than the permission religious people give one another to believe things strongly without evidence, a conflict between science and religion is unavoidable.

Religion and science are also in conflict because there is no way of disentangling religious and scientific truth-claims: the belief that Jesus was born of a virgin may be central to the doctrine of Christianity, but it is also an explicit claim about biology; the belief that Jesus will physically return to earth in the future entails a variety of claims about history, the human survival of death, and, apparently, the mechanics of human flight without the aid of technology. It is time that all rational people acknowledged that where claims about the nature of reality are concerned, there is only one magisterium.

The Empty Wager

The fundamental problem with religion is that it is built, to a remarkable degree, upon lies. I refer not merely to twenty-megaton displays of hypocrisy, as when Evangelical preachers get caught with male prostitutes or methamphetamine (or both). Rather, I refer to the daily and ubiquitous failure of most religious people to admit that the basic claims of their faith are profoundly suspect. Mommy claims to know that Granny went straight to heaven after she died. But Mommy doesn't actually know this. The truth is that Mommy is lying—either to herself or to her children—and most of us have agreed to view this behavior as perfectly normal. Rather than teach our children to grieve and to be happy despite the reality of death, we nourish their powers of self-deception.

How likely is it that Jesus was really born of a virgin, rose from the dead, and will bodily return to earth at some future date? How reasonable is it to believe in such a concatenation of miracles on the basis of the Gospel account? How much support do these doctrines receive from the average Christian's experience in church? Honest answers to these questions should raise a tsunami of doubt. I'm not sure what will be "Christian" about any Christians left standing.

Many readers of *Letter to a Christian Nation* have taken inspiration from Blaise Pascal and argued that evidence is beside the point and that religious believers have simply taken the wiser of two bets: if a believer is wrong about God, there is not much harm to him or to anyone else, and if he is right, he wins eternal happiness; if an atheist is wrong, however, he is destined to spend eternity in hell. On this view, atheism is the very picture of reckless stupidity.

While Pascal deserves his reputation as a brilliant mathematician, his wager was never more than a cute (and false) analogy. Like many cute ideas in philosophy, it is easily remembered and often repeated, and this has lent it an undeserved air of profundity. A moment's thought reveals that if the wager were valid, it could justify almost any belief system, no matter how ludicrous or antithetical to Christianity. Another problem with the wager—and it is a problem that infects religious thinking generally—is its suggestion that a rational person can knowingly will himself to believe a proposition for which he has no evidence. A person can *profess* any creed he likes, of course, but to really believe it, he must believe that it is true. To believe that there is a God, for instance, is to believe that you are not just fooling yourself; it is to believe that you stand in some relation to God's existence such that, if He didn't exist, you wouldn't believe in him. How does Pascal's wager fit into this scheme? It doesn't.

The reasons to doubt the existence of God are in plain view for everyone to see: everyone can see that the Bible is not the perfect word of an omniscient deity; everyone can see that there is no evidence for a God who answers prayers, and that any God who would grant prayers for football championships, while doling out cancer and car accidents to little boys and girls, is unworthy of our devotion. Everyone who has eyes to see *can* see that if the God of Abraham exists, He is an utter psychopath—and the God of Nature is too. If you can't see these things just by looking, you have simply closed your eyes to the realities of our world.

I have no doubt that many Christians find great consolation in their faith. But faith is not the best source of consolation. Faith is like a pickpocket who loans a person his own money on generous terms. The victim's gratitude is perfectly understandable, but absolutely misplaced. *We* are the source of the love that our priests and pastors attribute to God (how else can we feel it?). Your own consciousness is the cause and substance of any experience you might want to deem "spiritual" or "mystical." Realizing this, what possible need is there to pretend to be certain about ancient miracles?

Sam Harris
September 2007
New York

TEN BOOKS I RECOMMEND

1. *The God Delusion* by Richard Dawkins
2. *Breaking the Spell* by Daniel C. Dennett
3. *Misquoting Jesus* by Bart D. Ehrman
4. *Kingdom Coming* by Michelle Goldberg
5. *The End of Days* by Gershom Gorenberg
6. *Freethinkers* by Susan Jacoby
7. *Extraordinary Popular Delusions and the Madness of Crowds* by Charles Mackay
8. *Why I Am Not a Christian* by Bertrand Russell
9. *God, the Devil, and Darwin* by Niall Shanks
10. *Atheism: The Case Against God* by George H. Smith

NOTES

Commandments on public property (http://pew forum.org/press/index.php?ReleaseID=32).

26 The vaccine produced: "Forbidden Vaccine," *The New York Times*, Dec. 30, 2005 (editorial).

27 One study found: M. Goldberg, *Kingdom Coming: The Rise of Christian Nationalism* (New York: W. W. Norton, 2006), p. 137.

28 The rate of gonorrhea: N. D. Kristof, "Bush's Sex Scandal," *The New York Times*, February 16, 2005.

28 Reginald Finger: M. Specter, "Political Science," *The New Yorker*, March 13, 2006, pp. 58–69.

32 In fact, several states: "The States Confront Stem Cells," *The New York Times*, March 31, 2006.

32 If one experiments: www.usccb.org/prolife/issues/ bioethic/statelaw.htm.

35 Christopher Hitchens: "Mommie Dearest," 10/20/03, www.slate.com/id/2090083/.

36 "The greatest destroyer": http://nobelprize.org/ peace/laureates/1979/teresa-lecture.html.

37 In El Salvador: J. Hitt, "Pro-Life Nation," *The New York Times Magazine*, April 9, 2006.

38 20 percent: C. P. Griebel et al., "Management of Spontaneous Abortion," *American Family Physician*, vol. 72, no. 7 (October 1, 2005), pp. 1243–50.

42 The Vatican itself: J. I. Kertzer, "The Modern Use of Ancient Lies," *The New York Times*, May 9, 2002.

43 According to the United Nations': P. Zuckerman, "Atheism: Contemporary Rates and Patterns," in *The Cambridge Companion to Atheism,* Michael Martin, ed. (Cambridge, Eng.: Cambridge University Press, forthcoming).

44 The same comparison: G. S. Paul. "Cross-National

Correlations of Quantifiable Societal Health with Popular Religiosity and Secularism in the Prosperous Democracies," *Journal of Religion and Society,* vol. 7 (2005); R. Gledhill, "Societies Worse Off 'When They Have God on Their Side,' " *The Times* (U.K.), September 27, 2005.

44 **While political party affiliation:** http://people-press.org/commentary/display.php3?AnalysisID=103.

45 **Of the twenty-five:** www.morganquitno.com/cit06pop.htm#25.

45 **three of the five most dangerous:** www.fbi.gov/ucr/ucr.htm.

45 **Of the twenty-two:** www.itaffectsyou.org/blog/?p=200.

46 **Countries with high levels:** www.globalissues.org/TradeRelated/Debt/USAid.asp#ForeignAidNumbers inChartsandGraphs; www.oecd.org.

46 **Consider the ratio:** www.nybooks.com/articles/17726.

48 **"not in the power":** www.thetablet.co.uk/sample04.shtml.

57 **we know on the basis of textual evidence:** See J. Pelikan, *Jesus Through the Centuries* (New York: Harper & Row, 1987); A. N. Wilson, *Jesus: A Life* (New York: W. W. Norton, 1992); and B. M. Metzger and M. D. Coogan, eds., *The Oxford Companion to the Bible* (Oxford, Eng.: Oxford University Press, 1993), pp. 789–90.

58 **The Gospels also contradict:** There are many secondary sources that point out such contradictions. Burr's *Self-contradictions of the Bible* (1860) is a classic.

62 **"At the root"**: National Academy of Sciences, *Teaching About Evolution and the Nature of Science* (1998), p. 58; www.nap.edu/catalog/5787.html.

70 **Meanwhile, high school students in the United States:** L. Gross, "Scientific Illiteracy and the Partisan Takeover of Biology," PLoS Biol 4(5): e167. DOI: 10.1371/journal.pbio.0040167 (2006); http://biology.plosjournals.org/perlserv?request=get-document&doi=10.1371/journal.pbio.0040167.